# JUGGALO COUNTRY

# JUGGALO COUNTRY

## Inside the World of Insane Clown Posse and America's Weirdest Music Scene

**CRAVEN ROCK**

ILLUSTRATED BY **DAMON THOMPSON**

**Microcosm Publishing**
**Portland, Oregon**

# JUGGALO COUNTRY

## Inside the World of Insane Clown Posse and America's Weirdest Music Scene

© Craven Rock, 2013, 2019

This edition © Microcosm Publishing 2019

First published August 12, 2019

ISBN 978-1-62106-318-6

This is Microcosm #211

Edited by Elly Blue

Photos by Greg Clarke Photography, 2017

Illustrations by Damon Thompson, 2013, 2019

Cover and design by Joe Biel

**To join the ranks of high-class stores that feature Microcosm titles, talk to your local rep:** In the U.S. **Como** (Atlantic), **Fujii** (Midwest), **Book Travelers West** (Pacific), **Turnaround** in Europe, **UTP/Manda** in Canada, **New South** in Australia, and **Baker & Taylor GPS** in Asia, Africa, India, and other countries.

For a catalog, write or visit:

Microcosm Publishing

2752 N Williams Ave.

Portland, OR 97227

www.Microcosm.Pub

If you bought this on Amazon, I'm so sorry because you could have gotten it cheaper and supported a small, independent publisher at www.Microcosm.Pub

Global labor conditions are bad, and our roots in industrial Cleveland in the 70s and 80s made us appreciate the need to treat workers right. Therefore, our books are MADE IN THE USA.

*Library of Congress Cataloging-in-Publication Data*

Names: Rock, Craven, author.

Title: Juggalo Country : inside the world of Insane Clown Posse and America's weirdest music scene / Craven Rock.

Description: Second edition. | Portland, OR : Microcosm Publishing, [2018]

Identifiers: LCCN 2018041763 | ISBN 9781621063186 (pbk.)

Subjects: LCSH: Insane Clown Posse (Musical group)--Influence. | Juggalos (Music fans) | Subculture--United States.

Classification: LCC ML421.I535 R63 2018 | DDC 782.421649--dc23

LC record available at https://lccn.loc.gov/2018041763

# MICROCOSM · PUBLISHING

Microcosm Publishing is Portland's most diversified publishing house and distributor with a focus on the colorful, authentic, and empowering. Our books and zines have put your power in your hands since 1996, equipping readers to make positive changes in their lives and in the world around them. Microcosm emphasizes skill-building, showing hidden histories, and fostering creativity through challenging conventional publishing wisdom with books and bookettes about DIY skills, food, bicycling, gender, self-care, and social justice. What was once a distro and record label was started by Joe Biel in his bedroom and has become among the oldest independent publishing houses in Portland, OR. We are a politically moderate, centrist publisher in a world that has inched to the right for the past 80 years.

*These stories are based on true events of the author's experiences, although some names have been changed for privacy.*

## ACKNOWLEDGMENTS

Thanks: Ryan Bearcan, Josh James Amberson, Alexis Wolf, Gina Siciliano, Chris Terry for editing help and putting up with me freaking out. Kayla Greet for editing hours of Gathering interviews, may you never find the land of candy. Writing and moral support from my Mad & Manic friends Michele and Jordan, my Olytopia family, my Northwest Family and everybody who bugged me about it. KC, Kieran Harrison, Caleb Thompson and Jake Uitti and the rest of Monarch Review for all their support. And of course, Damon Thompson for the adventure, ideas, and illustrations.

Dedicated to the Juggalos with the best of intentions.

# TABLE OF CONTENTS

# INTRODUCTION TO THE SECOND EDITION

"**W**oo!" the Juggalo in the way-oversized Hatchetman shirt and basketball shorts keeps shouting, in the fashion of wrestler Brett Hart. I know this because every now and then he says, "gimme a Brett Hart!"

My head pounds with sinus pain aggravated by each pothole or bump my bike hit on the way to the club, so I'm having a hard time with this good-natured, drunken Juggalo as he tries to get the still mostly empty club going.

He demands a "*Woo!*" out of everybody.

"Guy on the stage! *Woo!*"

"Juggalo over there. *Woo!*"

"You! Guy in the hat! *Woo!*"

"Bouncer guy, gimme a Brett Hart, *Woo!*"

The reactions to him range from patronizing to good humor.

A beefy bouncer with a shaved head and a goatee beside me chuckles and slaps me on the back saying, "It's going to be a wild night," before walking off. Later on, he'll tell me that he's worked many Juggalo shows and would prefer them over plenty of other crowds.

"You see how he's all obnoxious right now, but when he comes up to talk to us he's really polite," he says of the woo-shouting Juggalo, then shakes his head and laughs.

The show is Anybody Killa (ABK), a Native American Juggalo rapper who stood out to me on Psychopathic Records for putting a Native twist on the Dark Carnival—the Juggalo's Judeo-Christian-based faith—and for being badass enough to not only rap with a lisp but to wreck the mic as well. This is the first time I've rubbed shoulders with the Juggalos since I went to research this book at the Gathering Of The Juggalos way back in 2010.

As the poorly-attended show fills to a maximum of thirty to fifty people, it's an example of the unity and diversity of the Juggalo Family. A long-haired, grey-bearded, O.G Juggalo in his fifties passes a joint to a young, Latino break dancer in wicked clown face paint while explaining to me the ongoing feud between Insane Clown Posse (ICP) and number two Juggalo group, Twiztid. An older woman gushes at how excited she is to see ENASNIMAI ('I am in insane' spelled backward), as the man she came with, a broad biker-looking fellow, snaps photos of her with the horrorcore group outside the show. "I'm a grandma!" She makes a point of saying.

The bill is an odd one. An industrial band growls and beats on metal with a wrench. A completely out-of-place alternative band plays Smashing Pumpkins riffs over lush keyboards. A hardcore punk band gets in the faces of the 'los, shouting and pointing fingers, calling out "*Whoop! Whoop!*" He declares his excitement at getting to perform for them.

A curtain is drawn before ABK comes out, revealing a stage set of an ominous, dingy, urban liquor store like you'd find in his hometown of Detroit. A man playing a shopkeeper in an all-white uniform and apron sweeps the floor as a smoke machine further sets the tone. The Juggalos shout, "*Whoop! Whoop!*" as the beat of the track kicks in. ABK doesn't waste any time bursting on the stage in his clown makeup and spitting for a small but ecstatic bunch of Juggalos.

It almost seems like nothing has changed since my dive into the Juggalo's world half a decade ago, but just about everything has.

·     ·     ·

While some of the mystery around Juggalos has dissipated for me, my fascination was quickly rekindled when I saw how much Juggalo culture had changed over time. I'm not alone in this fascination. People still get excited and dumbfounded to hear I wrote a book about Juggalos. At the time of writing, I was surprised one hadn't already been written. After all, this is only a massive, underground subculture that paint their faces like sinister, macabre clowns and followed Insane Clown Posse (ICP) and other rappers on their label Psychopathic Records who rhymed about grisly murder and violence. A group that follows a faith they called the Dark Carnival, its gospel laid out in murder rhymes by ICP. These Juggalos, whose church is an ICP show where they are literally hosed down with hundreds of gallons of the generic soda, Faygo.

But there was a subtext to my fascination: my affinity for the underdog. Before I attended the 11<sup>th</sup> Annual Gathering of the Juggalos in 2010, I found their aesthetics off-putting, stopping short of revulsion, but I also saw a lot I was familiar with. The Juggalos were the underclass, not unlike people I came up around in small town America. They were poor and destitute, and they owned that. They let it all hang out and took pride in who they were. Everybody hated them and made fun of them, but they really didn't give a fuck. They were often the kind of people who looked out for each other and made efforts to befriend me and my illustrator. After I left, I found myself defending them.

At the time I signed the contract for this second edition, so much had changed in the Juggalo world. Back in 2010 there was little talk about the FBI labeling them as a "hybrid gang." It had just happened and it seemed the Juggalos failed to see the seriousness of it. As much as I like to consider myself a radical, I failed to see the seriousness of it myself. Over the years, the Juggalos would see more and more repression from the State for simply enjoying the music they like with their friends. Juggalos got kicked out of the military and lost government jobs. Police profiled and targeted them. They received higher sentencing for having Juggalo tattoos. One woman would even have her kids taken away. The FBI, like me, saw how Juggalos were outcast, hated, and looked down upon by just about everybody. They figured nobody would speak up for them, that nobody would come to their defense.

But the Juggalos resisted.

On September 16, 2017, when 3,000 Juggalos marched on Washington, I was rooting for them the whole way. It warmed my heart to see thousands of them sticking it to the Man. Clutching signs worded with phrases well thought out beforehand, like *"Don't shoot! I'm just a music fan with a really big family," "Faygo not Fascism," "Clown the police state," "Your music could be next,"* and my favorite, *"The FBI listens to Nickelback."* In a testament to the power of freedom, music, friendship and family, they dwarfed what was promoted as the alt-right's Mother of All Rallies, also happening on the double-booked National Mall—which peaked at 100-400 marchers.

Violent J, of the duo ICP, appropriately said the FBI's listing was "fascist and it's fucked up" when he called for the march. Soon Juggalo memes and agitprop were made with Leftist aesthetics. One meme pasted ICP's other half, Shaggy 2 Dope, in front of a red and black backdrop. Beside him was an Antifa logo, its black flag modified, adding the Juggalo's ubiquitous Hatchetman logo. To his left, the words to ICP's anti-racist song, "Your Rebel Flag," on which ICP rhymes, "rednecks call it pride, pride for what, white pride for slavery, it sickens my guts, I see that as a challenge, that you want to fight, you don't care who it offends, you say it's your right, well it's my right to sock you dead in your lip, fuck your rebel flag."

It's easy for me to see this as evidence of Juggalos getting woke. It's easy for me to see what they already represented—the true underclass and downtrodden as having revolutionary potential. But that's unfair to Juggalos, a largely apolitical group. Then again, in a sense, the Juggalos were always political. They always had a class consciousness and had it out for "richies."

They always rallied against bigotry in the form of racism and considered LGBTQ Juggalos a part of their Family.

·        ·        ·

Seizing the time, Struggalo Circus rose out of this environment in the Bay Area. Calling themselves "a ragtag and messy coalition between radicals and Juggalos," they saw the state's targeting of Juggalos as part of a larger struggle. Ape—one of Struggalo Circus' founders—told Renegade Media his feelings on the FBI repression, "It's more than just an issue for Juggalos. It's an issue for lots of smaller demographics and subgroups...If they can head check us and go after a group that nobody's going to defend right away, then it's easily setting a precedent for other groups. Then we can call them a gang, and then we can call them terrorists...It doesn't stop with us."

Struggalo Circus, like anti-fascists and the International Workers of the World who marched in solidarity with Juggalos on September 16, saw it all as one fight. Ape started Struggalo Circus with Kitty Stryker after the two met on a dating website. Stryker, new to the Juggalo Family after being introduced by Ape, was a longtime anarchist and community organizer. As a politicized sex worker, Stryker was familiar with police abuse. So she took a cue from the sex worker community who'd made pamphlets teaching police how to treat sex workers in a more humane way and Struggalo Circus set out to make a similar one for the police on how to deal with Juggalos in a less oppressive, prejudiced manner. They did this not seeking the blessing of the police, but for harm reduction.

The intersectionality of all oppressed groups came as no surprise for members of Struggalo Circus. As the gentrification of the Bay Area by the tech industry displaces thousands of residents, leaving many on the streets and in shantytowns, Struggalo Circus has also been working with the homeless community, a large number of whom are Juggalos, according to Stryker.

Ice-T once said of the Gathering of the Juggalos, "If this shit was political they'd shut it down." Maybe he was implying there was revolutionary potential to the Juggalos. If so, Struggalo Circus has taken up that gauntlet.

•          •          •

Right now, as I write, the alt-right, fascists and right-wing libertarians are using terms like freedom and free speech to push hateful and deadly agendas. As I write this, it hasn't been a year since they held a torch rally in Charlottesville, North Carolina, chanting, "Jews will not replace us" and attacking and beating up peaceful counter-protesters. When their event was shut down because of the resistance of these counter-protestors, James Alex Fields, Jr., a member of neo-Nazi group Vanguard America, drove his car into the crowd, wounding nineteen people and killing activist Heather Heyer. Their idea of freedom is based entirely around taking it away from others, a false front for authoritarianism. It's also one that's been legitimized by Donald Trump's white supremacist administration. When authoritarians and fascists are pushing freedom, it leads one to question what freedom really means.

I've heard feminists speak of the "freedom to move," meaning they deserve the right to go about their lives without fear of harassment or harm. Simple as it may be, it's still one that isn't granted to women.

At the Gathering, Juggalos talked about the freedom they felt there. For three days they were liberated from the outside world that didn't understand them, and they raved about how they could be free with their Family. And it was true; it was a wild, drug-addled, hedonistic bacchanal where there wasn't a lot you couldn't do. You couldn't throw shit at the wrestlers—well, you could, but your Family would chant, *"You fucked up!"* at you until you quit— but that was about the only thing you couldn't do.

Another thing about the Gathering in 2010 was the sleaze. It was the only place I've ever been where I've seen eleven-year-olds watching women oil wrestling without anybody thinking anything of it. Everywhere, you heard the non-stop chant of young 'los, *"Tit-ties! Tit-ties!"* Underneath tents, everywhere, women stripped and ground on poles. My experiences there were a constant conflict between my guilty pro-feminist conscience, and my id released in this trashy Babylon where I took it all in, in the name of gonzo journalism.

The high or low point of all this rampant misogyny— depending on who you are—was the Miss Juggalette Contest. This contest was hosted by porn star and career dirtbag, Ron Jeremy. He'd coerce young women to outdo each other in degrading acts before a drooling crowd of Juggalos. The contestants were judged on the strength of the Juggalos' cheering and it was the women who were the nastiest that got the loudest cheers. Rumor got back to me that the winner was a young woman who was sucking dollar bills off the dicks of audience members.

This was the environment that Rachel Paul went into in 2013, when she started 'Lettes Respect, a group of feminist

Juggalos. As an old school Juggalette, she'd been disgusted not by the sexuality of the event but how it had, under Ron Jeremy's direction, become cruel and degrading.

In an article for Faygolovers.net, she recalls,

"One time when the former Miss Juggalette host and ringleader Ron Jeremy asked a contestant, 'What's your talent?'

She said: 'I *love* video games! I'm great at them. I'm a total gamer and–'

He cut her short: 'That's boring.'

The crowd followed suit and booed her. She blushed.

Soon enough, the next girl grabbed the mike: 'Well…*I suck a mean dick!*'

And barely post-pubescent boys screamed wildly in approval. She may very well have started deep throating the microphone. Good for her. I didn't stick around to watch."

Paul had enough and decided to take the pageant back for the Juggalettes.

It's difficult, as an outsider, to understand Paul's belief that Juggalos can rise above this sexism. It seems like the Juggalo Family can only be a safe place for sexist men, because that's what their leadership has created. With ICP's influence over the Juggalos as charismatic leaders, I saw it as something completely entrenched in the culture. After all, ICP are shameless and over-the-top about their misogyny; I'd be hard-pressed to think of a time when they talked about a woman without calling her a bitch. Violent J's autobiography describes over the span of his life a deep hatred of women, from his younger days when he would violently assault sex workers, to one of the high points of his life, grabbing Sheryl Crow's butt backstage at Woodstock '99, boasting he did it "for all the scrubs."

It gets worse than a class rage butt grope. ICP's label Psychopathic Records got hit with 86 counts of sexual harassment taken up by their former entertainment lawyer, Andrea Pellegrini, who described her tenure as a "roller coaster of abuse" where she was almost continually harassed. Psychopathic Records staffer and Detroit DJ Dan Diamond, also known as Dirty Dan for his sleaziness, allegedly went as far as to bring Pellegrini and other women swag he'd pick up at adult entertainment events like dildos and "vagina tighteners."

In this environment, it's easy to see a hatred of women permanently yoked with Juggalo culture. However, Paul saw the potential for more in her Family. As a Juggalette who'd been there since she was a teenager, now in her 30's, she knew how much the Family cared for and respected each other. She remembered a time before the pageant was run by Ron Jeremy and Dirty Dan, when Juggalos were more open to seeing the contestants for who they were. When she went to work, she went to the very top. She contacted ICP's label, Psychopathic Records and popular Juggalo fansite, Faygolovers.net. She got Psychopathic to listen. Violent J's brother and booker Rob Bruce gave Ron Jeremy the boot (then took credit for it, of course, playing the chivalry card, saying, "In the middle of the Gathering I told him to go, and I put him on a plane"). And this is how 'Lettes Respect was born. Paul announced on Faygolovers.net that the contest would now be about who the contestants were, not how many preteen boners they could arouse from the audience. 'Lettes Respect then put together a gender diverse panel of judges to put that into effect. Contestants would be judged on more than mere sleaziness, while still allowing room for women who wanted to express their sexuality.

In the first round of the contest, Juggalettes talked about who they were without fear of being berated by porn stars. The second round was about their talents. And the final category was a swimsuit competition, but one that celebrated different body types rather than a race to see who could get their tits out of them first.

The Juggalos were accepting of Juggalette feminism. After all, respect is a word that the Juggalos kick around a lot. When I was there it usually came out in the form of base chivalry, rather than anything progressive, when it came to the treatment of women. But respect is respect and Clown Love is real, so a whole lot of Juggalos were willing to open up and listen to what 'Lettes Respect had to say. It wasn't long before the Juggalos were making a space where trans Juggalettes felt safe competing in the pageant.

'Lettes Respect and Struggalo Circus are good examples of Juggalos decentralizing power from the top by empowering themselves. And it's nice to see. My biggest criticism of the Juggalos was their ardor for ICP, and the way many of them would give up so much of themselves to this leadership. What I liked was the Family. Their acceptance and compassion for each other. The fact that so many of them were a joy to be around.

That they took ownership of their poverty and took back the shame society had put upon them. When I left the Gathering I worried about being critical of their leadership, wondering if I would be seen as just another hater. After feeling Clown Love, I had some guilt writing critically about their hero, ICP. And now more than half a decade later, I continue to be impressed with the sheer kindness and decency that these violent horrorcore, Wicked Shit music fans are capable of. So with that to catch you up, here's my story about the time I spent with the Juggalos.

# DAYS AND NIGHTS IN THE DARK CARNIVAL

*I believe you can make forces of good and evil work for you, to get what you want.*

— G.G Allin

If you look for Cave-In-Rock on the map (that is, if anyone would bother to put it on a map), you would find it located in Southern Illinois—right where the state butts up against Indiana and Kentucky, an outpost where the Midwest meets the South, separated by the muddy Ohio River. It is the former home of indentured servants and horse thieves, passed down to their offspring who have been broken by construction work, disgraced by welfare, and mutated by meth; their stories and culture lost to landlessness and all the other indignities of the rural poor.

There, in August, when the air is thick with humidity, a gathering commences. For a former Hoosier and former Kentuckian like me, it's hard not to find it symbolic that this space is where the Gathering of the Juggalos takes place. But it is there where 20,000 Juggalos come together for a family reunion of a subculture made up of mostly poor, disenfranchised, and uneducated followers of the horrorcore rap group Insane Clown Posse (ICP).

I know this because I am attending this year's Gathering after a five-year-long obsession I've had with Juggalos. This obsession began when I moved to Seattle and started seeing young people running the streets dressed in baggy pants and t-shirts and with full clown paint on. They just seemed to be going about their everyday lives, which confused and compelled me at the time. I would later figure out that these young people were fans of ICP, a band from the nineties that rapped as evil clowns. A band I had forgotten about long ago. I was astounded to find out they were getting new, younger fans who were so dedicated. I became obsessed.

I remembered ICP as a duo of white rappers from Detroit, Violent J and Shaggy 2 Dope, who painted their faces like clowns with sharp and pointy edges that gave them a leering, menacing countenance. They rapped about violence and murder while they sprayed their audience down with Faygo, a generic soda brand from the Michigan area. Five or six years ago, this was all I could tell you about ICP. I remembered how ICP worked their whole outrageous shtick at the same time Gothic band Marilyn Manson shock-rocked the mainstream with their dark, industrial sound and gory, androgynous stage show—but ICP had long since dropped under my radar. The more I looked into it, the more I found out ICP hadn't faded away, but had grown in popularity. Because instead of being a pop sensation, they cleverly managed to build a mystique that would garner a cult following. At the time of writing this, two of their albums had gone platinum and five gold, many charted in Billboard, and their most recent album, *Bang! Pow! Boom!,* debuted at #4 on the Billboard 200 and #1 on the Billboard Top Independent Albums charts. They managed to do all this while being completely ignored by the mainstream media. They started a hugely successful label called Psychopathic Records, to which they've signed other rappers who also put on the clown makeup and rap, including Twiztid, Anybody Killa, and Blaze Ya Dead Homie. Their collective success is entirely due to their obsessive fans called the Juggalos. Pop stars, rap stars, and rock stars come and go, but the cult of the Wicked Clown continues to attract new followers and grow.

But why? What makes a band so completely unpopular to the mainstream (and even to underground rap fans) become such a huge cult phenomenon? Everybody I've talked to who's familiar with ICP finds their sound and macabre aesthetics off-putting, garish and corny. How does ICP continue to draw younger fans? How are they staying relevant? How does the Wicked Clown still draw and attract after all these years? It's 2011. The members of ICP are in their late-30s. What the fuck is this all about?

Their increasing popularity has a lot to do with their fans "getting it." Violent J and Shaggy 2 Dope are, in their own words, "the most hated band in the world," and have become successful by making their own dark and violent subgenre of rap music: Wicked Shit. All arguments for and against the quality and relevance of Wicked Shit aside, it's the evil darkness in the music that seems to attract one to become a Juggalo in the first place. From all the online research I compiled before my trip to the Gathering, I put together that Juggalos feel they're into something too edgy, too violent, and too offensive for the rest of the world. Their love of Wicked Shit unites the Juggalos collectively into what they call the Juggalo Family. Only fellow Juggalos understand Wicked Shit and this strengthens the bond and solidarity between them, making them Family. Kids who are already outcast and disenfranchised are no longer hated because they are too skinny, too fat, too ugly, too poor, or too uneducated. They become Juggalos and are marginalized simply because they are too "wicked," too edgy, and too extreme.

"Their recruiting rhetoric is a lot like skinheads," says Damon, my illustrator, after doing some research before our trip. "Never being alone. Someone always having your back." Damon spent much of his youth and early twenties as an anti-racist skinhead. He sees parallels between the two working class subcultures. Oi, the musical genre of skinheads, is rife with songs about sticking together, being hated and marginalized, but never walking alone. This is true, but unique to the "Fam" is the promise of "Clown Love." If one is "down with the Clown" they will get love from the Family—unconditionally. While there is a degree of unity and togetherness in any subculture, it seems much stronger in the Juggalo Family as there are fewer conditions and ethics to cause division, or at least more elusive and malleable ethics than found in other subcultures.

Juggalo ethics are taught by ICP on twelve albums known as the Joker's Cards. Each album represents a card and reveals more secrets of the Juggalo faith, also known as the Dark Carnival. According to Violent J, the Dark Carnival came to him in a vision. In the early nineties, when they called themselves the Inner City Posse, a gangsta rap group that was becoming popular in Detroit due to their own ceaseless promotion, Violent J experienced a vision—or what I might call a hallucination—of spirits and leering clowns, which led to the Dark Carnival. He felt he was told by these spirit ninjas to spread the word of the Dark Carnival on earth and to guide his followers in their path to reach Shangri-La, the afterlife of the Juggalos. (Confusingly, not only are Juggalos ICP fans and followers of the faith known as the Dark Carnival, they are also collectively known as the Dark Carnival.)

In all my research on ICP and the Juggalos, one thing I've never grasped is the Dark Carnival. It seems to be a chicken or the egg type of deal—I'm not sure if one knows they're a Juggalo because they instinctively pick up the spirituality in a bunch of songs about mutilation and serial killing, or if one forces themselves to cull something spiritual out of the lyrics because they feel the call to become a Juggalo. A layman like me finds nothing in these songs but violence and dismemberment mixed in with scatological tales of jerking off in someone's mac and cheese. Whatever the Dark Carnival may entail, this spiritual awakening remains crucial to the Juggalo Family.

# CARNIVAL GATES

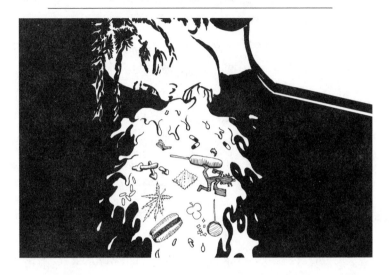

*On the perfect night dead people get to sleep in,*

*'Cause when they wake up on a night like this it's where to begin,*

*The ringmaster's wagons can travel far and undisturbed,*

*'Cept they show up in the dark for the town they about to serve...*

— Shaggy 2 Dope, "The Perfect Night"

We leave Louisville, Kentucky after dark, crossing over into Indiana. We're not too far before we've dipped completely into the blackness of Highway 64, the only lights coming from the occasional eastbound eighteen-wheeler. Fifteen miles over the border I see the truck stop sign near the exit leading to my teenage home, Milltown. My gut tightens as I think of that town—a town of meth and welfare and vicious brutality. When I left Milltown for Indianapolis, Insane Clown Posse was still Inner City Posse and just beginning to build up a rep in Detroit, and I was a punk rock kid with a poorly executed Mohawk and a chip on my shoulder. I don't remember there being any Juggalos in Milltown then.

My anxiety grows. Partially, it's fear of failure that eats at me—to come all the way out here to flop miserably at getting the Juggalo story. Maybe my anxiety has something to do with the Juggalos' reputation for violence, as well. Or it might just have something to do with passing the shitty small town that I grew up in, which is abstractly and subconsciously linked to my reason for making this trip.

There are no streetlights along the highway, just the long, black, rural Middle American night. So abysmal is the blackness that we're thankful for curves on the highway to break the monotony, for keeping sleep from sending us right off the road. All around us rural routes vein throughout the land leading to mobile homes and shacks where the forgotten live. If we drove down these gravel roads at any hour after dark, we would see lights in the windows, the residents inside wide awake, twitchy on crystal meth and guarded by rottweilers and pit bulls and shotguns.

In the light of the dashboard Damon hits the search button on the radio dial. He's unusually cranky and silent as we drive, forced to leave on the fly after a bad day at work as a concierge. He leaves me alone to my thoughts as the country station—the only station for miles—fades out. The green LED numbers twirl, searching for another place to rest before finally stopping on a classic rock station. The cab fills with Axl Rose's trademark yowl ripping its way through "Paradise City." The song, in context to location, brings back memories of Guns N' Roses blaring out of blown-out speakers of grey-primed hoopties as they ceaselessly cruised my old town, until the engines finally gave up or the drivers drunkenly wrapped them around a tree.

How alienated I felt then; I desperately wanted out of there and wanted more. Living in such a fucked-up place filled me with despair. Everything slides into context as I think about how I found punk rock and how it exposed me to everything good and healthy that would happen in my life. It empowered me, politicized me, and provided an outlet for my anger toward all the awful things going on all around me. Punk rock ultimately taught me to fight for something—to do something more than knock somebody up and get stuck in a small town for the rest of my life. It all began by going out to my first punk rock show and feeling the energy of a room full of angry kids. It made me realize I wasn't so alone, like I could be a part of something.

That pissed-off energy from my youth makes me think of the ire and condescension punks and others in counter-culture exhibit toward the mere mention of Juggalos, and I can't help feeling it's a bit ironic. I too find the whole Juggalo aesthetic to be distasteful, from the sophomoric toilet humor of Wicked Shit to the eyesore aesthetics of Hatchet Gear (the Psychopathic Records clothing line) fashion. More importantly, on an ethical level, I'm grossed out by the materialism, misogyny, and anti-intellectualism prevalent in Juggalo culture.

But I can't help empathizing with the Juggalos. If I don't understand what Juggalos do, I think I can understand why they do it, and maybe it's this empathy that led me to come all the way out here. Or maybe I'm just waxing pretentious as I ride down I-64, forced to confront my past. Maybe it's just the oddness and esoteric nature of Juggalo culture I want figure out, to get a grasp and put some closure on a long obsession. Maybe I just want to give them a fair shake, something they rarely, if ever, receive. Insane Clown Posse is wealthy and successful enough to be treated with some respect every now and then, but the Juggalos rarely get anything other than hate outside of the Dark Carnival.

· · ·

After four hours of driving and another hour of getting lost, we find the obscure dirt road leading to Hogrock, the allegedly biker-owned land where the Gathering takes place. It's three o'clock in the morning when we finally pull in. The Gathering looks like a mutated, nightmarish state fair. There is a carnival midway where one can buy staples like elephant ears, corn dogs, and Jumbo Bitch Beaters (Juggalo for a large turkey leg). There are carnival games that no one seems to be playing, and near the Main Stage there is a Ferris Wheel and a rocket ride called the Saturn 6.

Tents are strewn haphazardly everywhere in the Big Baller campsites. Big Baller campsites include electricity and running water. They cost a few hundred dollars (not included in the ticket price), as opposed to the free camping in the parking lot outside the grounds where we're camped, but the Juggalos cut the cost down by overflowing each spot with all their friends. Big Baller sites aren't marked, reserved or designated; instead it's pay per vehicle. So one group of Juggalos pays to drive a vehicle in to stake out land, and then all their homies park outside, walk in to the grounds, and stake tents all around the paying friends' tent to split up the cost. This makes for a chaotic and boundless tent city, symbolic of the resourcefulness and devil-may-care-attitude of the Juggalos.

Some Juggalos are running around with glow sticks strapped all over themselves. Some are decked out in full Wicked Clown face paint. Even the entertainment is like a state fair lineup—washed-up groups from over 10 years ago, like Naughty By Nature and Above The Law. In the Freak Tent a band called Critical Bill plays really bad yo-metal that sounds as if it came out of a time warp from the mid-'90s. For non-musical entertainment, we can choose between big-dicked porn star Ron Jeremy doing stand-up comedy, or the premier of *Big Money Rustlas*, a Western movie made by Insane Clown Posse. It looks like any other Western, only Shaggy 2 Dope and Violent J's characters are done up in their clown makeup, while the rest of the cast just wear John Waynesque garb.

My feet nearly get run over by a golf cart as I distractedly sip on my beer. A chorus of "*Whoop! Whoop!*" goes up from the three seated Juggalos in the cart and the four hanging off the back. A sign on the back says, "rides $3.00 or tits." These carts constantly zig-zag through the grounds, even during the late hours.

"Hey ninja," I hear over my shoulder from a chubby female Juggalo in full face paint, as I recover from my near handicapping.

"Have you seen my Juggalette around here? Wearing a short skirt with big titties?" she asks.

Thus, my first conversation begins with a Juggalo after all these years of armchair internet research.

"Nah, I didn't. I'm sure that I'd notice something like that," I reply, looking away awkwardly.

"C'mon, ninja, you got them glasses on and shit," she teases dryly.

"Hey, y'all got the same shorts," Damon cuts in and laughs.

"Why you bitin' my style?" She wanders off in the other direction.

We cross the didactically named Drug Bridge to get to the Second Stage. Drug Bridge is 20 yards long and a couple of cars wide, and on it is a scene like no other—under streetlights dizzy with moths, Juggalos are balling every kind of drug imaginable...every kind of drug. Juggalos hock them fearlessly, using incriminating terms. Ecstasy. Cocaine. Ketamine. Xanax. Percocet. A lot of the dealers can't possibly be older than sixteen. They hold signs made from cardboard ripped from Faygo boxes and marked "Purple Kush $25," "Acid $10 a hit," and "Rolls $10." There are at least 60 people on the bridge—selling, buying, or just milling about socializing. The dealers all shout out what they have and it's a cacophonous din, reminding me of the sound of street vendors in Mexican markets, but even more disorderly. This lawlessness is one benefit to the Gathering being on private property—if the cops aren't called, the Juggalos manage to get away with everything.

Across the Drug Bridge and in the area called Scrub Central, we see the Second Stage where Afroman, a flash-in-the-pan from the early 2000s, sings his odes to pot and tall cans. Some of the crowd happily shout out the chorus to "I Got High," while others launch water balloons at him. He's getting Clown Love.

A Juggalo near me chucks a plastic bottle at the stage, and a mustached guy in a yellow jacket shines a Maglite on him. He's probably Afroman's own personal security, because he's the only security I see all week besides those guarding ICP on the main stage. The Juggalo then gets his own flashlight and shines it in the yellow-jacketed man's face for the rest of the set. The security guard grows angrier while the Juggalo and his crew laugh at him. It's a clear representation of who holds the power at the Gathering and helps ground me to where I'm going to be for the next four days. Lawlessness is the rule.

After Afroman's set, we cross back over the Drug Bridge and a guy decked out in Hatchet Gear shouts out, "five-dollar lines of coke!" His crew, also wearing Hatchet Gear, surround him.

Damon reaches in my backpack, which contains only toilet paper and tall cans of beer, grabs the T.P. and makes a stop at the third in a long line of spray-painted porta-potties. I notice the phrase "namaste sharts" in red paint as the door closes.

"Somebody shit in the urinal," he says when he comes back out.

# MIRACLE AT HOGROCK

*We don't have to be high to look in the sky,*

*And know that's a miracle opened wide,*

*Look at the mountains, trees, the seven seas,*

*And everything chilling underwater, please,*

*Hot lava, snow, rain and fog,*

*Long neck giraffes, and pet cats and dogs.*

> – Insane Clown Posse, "Miracles"

Insane Clown Posse went viral not long ago and gained quite a bit of notoriety. Haters poked fun at the video for their song "Miracles," an anti-intellectual, quasi-Christian homage to nature in which Violent J and Shaggy 2 Dope gush with the rapture of a couple of blissed-out E-tards about stuff like long-necked giraffes "fucking rainbows and dirt," and proclaim them miracles. At one point Shaggy asks, "fucking magnets, how do they work?" before boldly stating, "and I don't wanna talk to a scientist, y'all motherfuckers lyin' and gettin' me pissed," while Violent J makes the case that "music is all magic, it's just there in the air," as he gazes loftily and thoughtfully into the stars through his clown makeup. Even if you could get over Shaggy's anti-intellectualism and chose to accept the song as an almost Whitmanesque embrace of the wonders of life and the universe, it would be hard not to admit that it's a ridiculous, corny song—so corny that it received millions of hits on YouTube based on mockery alone.

Around the same time, *Saturday Night Live* parodied a YouTube infomercial that Insane Clown Posse and Psychopathic Records had made to promote the 10th Gathering of the Juggalos. While it was a noble effort for *SNL*, whose skit went as far as promising a helicopter spraying piss on the attendees, the real thing proved to be far more surreal because it *was* real. Psychopathic's infomercial promoted an absurd, trashy music festival—promising a guy being shot out of a cannon three times a day, " dudes on stilts," "ninjas spinning fire," wet t-shirt contests, "real" midway games, Love Train Hayrides, Hog Daddy's Hellfire of Death (with "Magicians and Hypnotists walking around that bitch"), Oddball Wrestling on glass and barbed wire "with midgets, ladies, oddities, and some of the most bizarre people in the world," Late Night Comedy with Upchuck The Clown and Pauly Shore, and plenty of outhouses. However unintentional, the *SNL* parody brought a lot of attention to the actual Gathering infomercial and helped turn the Juggalos into the household word they are to this day.

Part of the subculture's intrigue is in the fact that it's growing and getting stronger, not fading out like fads do. And it hasn't lost its appeal to young people, even as Violent J and Shaggy push forty. All the negative mainstream attention was bound to happen because the Juggalos were just getting too big to ignore.

•       •       •

From the Love Wagon, as it passes by, a skinny, young Juggalo pleads desperately to a well-endowed, thick Juggalette, "Oh, my God! I have to see those titties!"

She smiles shyly, looks to the right to her Juggalette friend and then down at the ground. The Love Wagon is basically a hay ride without the hay—a huge wood and metal trailer pulled by a John Deere tractor with about 30-plus Juggalos hanging all over it at any given time.

Damon gets nailed with a Faygo bottle hocked by one of the riders and we hear a chorus of *"Whoop! Whoop!"* He laughs, chucks it back, and we continue walking back to camp for more beer.

A guy who's sitting at a picnic table with his girlfriend says, "Nice shirt," to Damon about his Misfits t-shirt, which has already created a small controversy here. Some Juggalos give him shit for liking something other than Wicked Shit.

"Thanks," Damon says. "Want a beer?"

"Sure, if you can spare one," he says, and I sigh to myself.

"I'm Nathan," he continues, then shakes our hands.

The girl introduces herself as Samantha. They both look a little bit like indie rockers—Samantha has long blonde hair, blue eyes, and wears a vintage sundress complemented by home-crafted jewelry. Nathan is well shaven and has short black hair. He wears a pastel-blue t-shirt of an obscure band and blue jeans that fit. They aren't wearing Hatchet Gear, but what really makes them stand out is they're a gorgeous couple, by anybody's standards.

"We're from Portland," Nathan says.

"Which one?" I ask.

"Oregon."

I roll my eyes. They're from Portland, Oregon.

Nathan is the reason they're here. He's one of a rare breed—an Insane Clown Posse fan, but not a Juggalo. Nathan used to be really into ICP in his teens and still holds a soft spot for them, so they made the trip to see his old faves and to check out the craziness. We walk together; Damon's in one of his drunken raconteur moods, and by the time we arrive back at the van they're enthralled by tales of his anti-racist skinhead past and how he used to thump Nazis back in the day.

I follow Damon to the back of the van when he heads to the cooler.

"Get rid of them," I whisper to him.

If he hears me, he doesn't acknowledge it. I like them, but I imagine us just talking to the non-Juggalos we meet out here; I want to avoid other outsiders. I only want to talk to Juggalos. I want to get into the Juggalo mindset and just talk to the Family. We've already been approached by a journalist and a photographer who are here together. Like Nathan, they broke the ice with Damon's Misfits t-shirt. They wear press passes and are the real thing, but we want to stay scrubby.

I guess Nathan and Samantha are in their early twenties. Folks their age tend to find the Juggalos less bizarre or less mysterious for the simple fact they went to high school with some of them. It's really fascinating to think there might be a whole lunch table of Juggalos in some high schools now; when I was in high school, there weren't enough misfits to fill one table, let alone a whole crew claiming allegiance to one band.

If Nathan ever considered himself a Juggalo, he doesn't let on. What's relevant at this stage in his life is he's an un-ironic fan. He and Samantha *drove* all the way across the country to see this. Hell, these two are probably even crazier and weirder than we are to be out here—at least, we're not out here for entertainment. But entertained they are! They laugh when they tell us some of the things they've seen. They have a detached point of view, but aren't necessarily condescending. (Later on, after the Gathering ended, I wondered about what they do in Portland, what music they listen to now, what the hell they're all about, and if I'll ever run into them again.)

I don't let Damon know, but I'm glad to have met them. Damon made the right move. Getting to know Nathan and Samantha allows us to hear about some of the crazy stuff we'll miss at the Gathering, since we can't be everywhere at once. But I don't tell them I'm here to write about it.

Except for Nathan and Samantha, and the journalist and his photographer, we have yet to encounter another non-Juggalo. There may be a few journalists running around exploiting their backstage passes, but out here it seems there are 20,000 Juggalos and us. I take a whole lot of comfort in this. Due to all the hype about the "Miracles" video, I was expecting we might already be behind the curve and the Gathering would be overrun with ironic hipster bloggers. But it's not, and this gives me some peace of mind about our project. It also makes me feel more adventurous.

"Fuck it!" I think to myself while tossing my ancient tape recorder into the van. The damn thing is pretty much broken and at this point I'm kind of drunk, another example of how fly-by-night this project is. I come back around to where Damon sits, he looks at me and just busts out laughing.

"Dude, you don't fit in here at all," he laughs, "With that ridiculous hat, the journal pouch on your belt and your glasses and your shoes... Dude, nobody here is wearing Converse."

"Fuck you," I say, smile, and throw my hat into the van with dramatized frustration.

I grab the tape recorder again. It's at least been working some of the time. We head back inside the gates.

Damon's and my plan was to throw proper journalism to the wind and just do what the Juggalos do—meet folks, possibly make friends, and avoid the detached distance other journalists approach their subjects with. Getting drunk is something we both spend a lot of time doing anyway, when we're not working on our craft and sometimes even when we are. We may not do everything the Juggalos do, but this one's easy.

Wanting to start somewhere with my questions for the Juggalos, I decide the Dark Carnival is a good place. I figure I'll ask what the Dark Carnival means to them, and see where it goes from there. I've got a healthy buzz, not totally shitfaced. I'm with my best friend in the world, and the sun is going down, and the air is still thick with grape blunts—a sweet smell I'm sure will forever trigger the Gathering for me. I feel positive as we walk; it's as good a starting point as any.

I start thinking about Damon, and how glad I am to have him along. His coming was an accident, but possibly one of the only things I did right in my preparation. I only called Damon to tell him that I was going to be flying into Louisville soon on my way to the Gathering of the Juggalos, and asked him jokingly, "Wanna go?"

"No," he said firmly. "Of course I don't want to go."

I could hear the laughter of some of his friends in the background. I laughed, then still joking, asked, "What if I paid?"

"Maybe, if you paid," he said.

I hung up the phone and thought about it. Damon would be the perfect guy to take with me. I called him the next day and he agreed to come.

At first, my purpose for bringing him would be as my illustrator, but he came in handy in a lot of other ways. For instance, basic safety—I had no clue what I was getting myself into or what it would be like. While it could all be just a lot of hype, Juggalos have a reputation for being violent. Not being at the Gathering totally alone was definitely something to take into consideration. I went from having to hitchhike out to the middle of nowhere, trying to figure how to camp with just a backpack without getting all my shit stolen, to riding in a van with my best friend and having someone to bounce observations off of and to run around and get drunk with. It's a hell of a lot better than wandering around by myself, awkwardly trying to mingle.

We're really comfortable around each other, and that makes other people comfortable around us. Damon is an easy, fun guy to be around; he's an enormous brawler, but he's also good at listening to people and empathizing with them. He doesn't suffer fools lightly, but he genuinely struggles to respect the flawed animal that is humanity, despite how much it conflicts with his intelligence.

I could go on about the complexities of Damon. Overall, I couldn't ask for a better companion out here, except for the fact that he's struggling with intense pain in his left foot. This changes the game a bit, and I spend a lot of time running around taking things in by myself. When he gets back from the Gathering he finds out that he has gout, a disease that is triggered and escalated by heavy drinking.

# WICKED SHIT 101

*The more haters you have in your life, the fresher you are.*

– Violent J

To understand the nuances of Juggalo life, it may be a good idea to explore the subtle differences in the music they listen to: Wicked Shit and horrorcore. First of all, Wicked Shit and horrorcore are similar. They both use gory and macabre imagery—lyrics of stabbings, beheadings, and if-you-fuck-with-me-I'll-brutally-murder-you themes. Horror films strongly influence both. However, they are not synonymous; all Wicked Shit can be called horrorcore, but not all horrorcore can be called Wicked Shit. Horrorcore is much less of a cult phenomenon than Wicked Shit and exists more as a subgenre of hip hop than a scene that stands alone. Respectable MCs and producers have associated with horrorcore. For instance, *Dr. Octagonecologyst* is considered by many to be a classic hip hop album, but few would think of it as a horrorcore record, even though Dr. Octagon—aka Kool Keith, a well-respected and critically-acclaimed MC—does and has gone as far as saying he invented the style. OG, Brooklyn producer, Prince Paul, and RZA of Wu-Tang were part of the horrorcore group Gravediggaz, long after making their names in hip hop.

If anyone blends the two terms Wicked Shit and horrorcore, it is usually the Juggalos, not fans of horrorcore. Wicked Shit, from my narrow understanding, is made by and for the Juggalos. Basically, one expects some Wicked Clown involvement (or at least a huge tolerance for greasepaint) with anything dubbed Wicked Shit. More than likely a group playing Wicked Shit clowns up on stage and alludes to the Dark Carnival and Shangri-La in their lyricism. It's associated with ICP. Wicked Shit is a term used almost exclusively by the Juggalos. It can also be argued that Wicked Shit is religious or spiritual music, because generally it teaches the way of the Dark Carnival.

Another thing that stands out with Wicked Shit is its sense of humor. For all of its violent lyrics there is a less serious tone, one that doesn't mesh well with the rest of hip hop, a genre that can take itself far too seriously. Even horrorcore plays it pretty straight. Gravediggaz and groups like them are always mean-mugging' and glowering from their album covers as if to demand respect, but possibly betraying insecurity. Wicked Clowns may be wicked, but they're still clowns. A lot of times there's also heavy metal crossover to Wicked Shit's instrumentation, which also doesn't necessarily mesh with the rest of hip hop. These things also seem to appeal to a whiter, underclass audience, further distancing it from the rest of rap.

I've met some Juggalos who have more eclectic musical tastes, but there's a puritanism to most of them. Some only listen to horrorcore, some filter out everything but Wicked Shit. A huge portion of Juggalos only listen to Psychopathic Records groups. And it gets narrower. A lot of Juggalos I meet seem to only listen to ICP with maybe the exception of Twiztid.

As a subculture they may be accepting to outsiders, but their adherence, and perhaps close-mindedness, to anything but their own musical genre is crucial because it strengthens the bonds of the group. For instance, when the Juggalos mock Damon's Misfits t-shirt, it's not necessarily because they think The Misfits are a shitty band, more likely because The Misfits don't play Wicked Shit. Juggalos feel what they're into is too subversive, underground, and profane for the masses to understand, and as much as their haters may balk, there's a lot more truth to it than they think. Hip haters and non-Juggalos think ICP's music is corny or puerile. They think all ICP's songs are laughable, even when they are trying to be spiritual. What the Juggalos get that outsiders don't, despite being glaringly obvious, is…the joke. ICP is trying to be funny, they are trying to entertain. Their humor is stupid and pedestrian, but the Juggalos know this. They're okay with it. They want to have a good time. The same goes for all the violence. Juggalos understand the violent themes as simply a healthy way to deal with the stress and aggression of the underclass. You could say the same thing about The Misfits, but you could never get away with saying they don't take themselves seriously. Juggalos don't get a lot of credit for understanding their own music and culture. Perhaps it's because shit-talking non-Juggalos don't get the nuance of Wicked Shit and don't want to admit that there's anything there for them not to get. Haters want to mock the Juggalos for being marginalized, but the Juggalos are proud of being insular.

ICP is able to capitalize on this insularity. Even though they are total hip hop heads themselves, a taste reflected in their booking at The Gathering ('90s rappers that haven't been relevant since their youth), they give something entirely different to the Juggalos with Wicked Shit. With Wicked Shit, ICP are able to isolate the Juggalos from everything else. ICP benefits greatly from the Juggalos' seclusion, and are able to further manipulate their niche market into buying merchandise and supporting their tours. This isolationism also informs my fascination with the Juggalos. They exist in a cultural vacuum, either mocked or ignored by the rest of rap culture, which they gloat only makes them stronger. In addition to this, they are cut off from counter-cultural lineage altogether.

As much as the different affiliations within modern subculture may not get along smoothly, they all come from a long thread of resistance. Punk said, "never trust a dirty hippie," but it was a reaction against the stoned, drop-out culture the 60s hippie movement turned into. At heart, punk and hippie shared a lot of the same ethics. How far it goes back is not something that I care to get into here, but the style and fashion of counter-culture, from hip hop to punk to the black-clad anarchists, each carry their own cultural alchemy, all of which is linked to something else. The Wicked Clown aesthetic doesn't trigger this alchemy or this historical memory of resistance, resulting in coming across as garish and repulsive to the rest of counterculture. For example, I may have vastly different tastes than some of my raver friends who listen to electronic music, but we can come together under an umbrella of radicalism or DIY politics. The Juggalo in the clown makeup stands alone… with his Family. This helps explain why the Juggalos are such a shock and a mystery to the rest of counter-culture. Juggalos gross out punks, they offend or induce pity from anarchists and radicals, ironic hipsters make fun of them, and the rest of hip hop pretend they don't exist. But few members of these groups actually know any Juggalos, and they remain a mystery to them. In my short time at The Gathering I developed a bit of sympathy for the Juggalos. Despite my snobbishness, I feel that they came to the Family for the same reason that anyone would join any subculture: to be empowered, to be a part of something bigger than themselves, to belong.

·          ·          ·

I wake up when it starts to get hot in the van. It's early in the morning and already muggy. Damon has been up and wandering around and now he draws in the front seat of the van; he turns around and shows me the picture.

"Look what I saw this morning," he says with a grin, "a bunch of naked girls hanging off the back of a golf cart."

He sets his sketchbook down, we grab a jug of water and head back out into the madness.

It doesn't take long for us to ease into The Gathering. Looking around at the crowd, I feel less intimidated than I did yesterday on the way in. Most of the crowd looks like the same crustached and goateed poor white folks I grew up around, except they are decked out in Hatchet Gear. As Damon bluntly puts it, "They've managed to bring together the redneck and the wigger." I may have left the shitty towns of my youth behind long ago, but I still remember the desperation of folks there—the simmering rage that would come out in bursts of violence upon people who didn't even know how they disrespected them. A phrase comes to mind, one I've often heard repeated in jest by the non-Juggalo: "Don't fuck with a Juggalo." But still, let me say at the risk of watering down the drama or making our mission seem less intrepid: we've encountered little trouble at The Gathering because we've shown respect.

We pass several camps as we walk the trail. Homemade banners display where each party hails from. Bed sheets bear names like Grimtown, VA, Camp Chaos, and Bay Area Ninjas in permanent marker, surrounded by logos of Wicked Shit bands and Insane Clown Posse's ubiquitous Hatchetman logo—a cartoonish silhouette of a dreadlocked man running with a Hatchet. There are also plenty of professionally done banners people shelled out quite a bit for, just for some hometown pride. Beat-up cars covered in Psychopathic Records stickers litter the grounds, along with rented RVs. Every now and then we see a customized hot rod or lowrider—sleek, glittery, and proudly proclaiming Wicked Clown affiliation with their design. Most of the camps sell cans of Faygo, hot dogs, glow sticks, glow-in-the-dark hatchets, loosies, shots of whiskey, Jell-O shots, or cans of beer. Scrawled cardboard signs advertising these wares hang on poles and trees around each camp. Unlike a punk fest or hippie gathering, and true to their hip hop roots out here, it's all balls-out hustling. Everyone is doing it. Some Juggalos even thought to bring things like batteries and bags of ice to sell at a profit. The Juggalos are generally pretty fair, though; cans of beer don't go for much more than a dollar. It's laissez-faire capitalism combined with a respect for Family.

The sweet grape scent of blunts, carnival food, and the loud call and response of *"Whoop! Whoop!!"* permeate the humid air. *"Whoop! Whoop!'* is the cry of the Juggalo. They use it to convey many things: they shout it out as greeting, they shout it out when they're drunk, they shout it out when they're high, and they shout it out to let everyone know that they're a down-ass 'lo having a good time. Exactly how important the chant is becomes clear at about 10:00 am on our first morning as we walk through Spazzmatic.

Spazzmatic acts as a bar/social area—a sort of cabana where picnic tables surround a wooden bar, behind which a chunky Juggalette serves nothing but Faygo and a few snacks. Hiding in the shade from the blazing sun, Juggalos kick it on the picnic tables, catching up on the last year and talking about representing the Hatchet in their town. When we walk in, a scraggly-goateed, long-haired white kid, shirtless and wearing Hatchet Gear basketball shorts, sticks out his fist to give me knucks. I give him his dap and he grins. As we move through the tables, Juggalos continue to converse amongst each other like any bar or party or lunchroom scenario, except every couple of minutes someone calls out *"Whoop! Whoop!"* and the whole vicinity answers back, *"Whoop! Whoop!"* Then they turn back to their conversations. A few minutes later it happens again: *"Whoop! Whoop!"* We quickly work this phrase into our vocabulary.

A common chant besides *"Whoop! Whoop!"* is *"Family!"* Each syllable pronounced with deep-throated inflection so it comes out, *"Fam-uh-lee!"* Hearing large groups of Juggalos echo it all around reminds me that I don't belong here, and it unsettles me. There's a nonverbal Juggalo signifier in their hand sign—a complicated twisting of their fingers into what I finally figure out is supposed to be "WC" for the Wicked Clown.

A proper way to greet a Juggalo or a Juggalette (a female Juggalo) is to say the shortened "'lo" or "'lette." But there's also "ninja," as in, "what up, ninja?" At first, I thought this might be a way for a white rap group to put a twist on the N-word without perpetrating, but according to Violent J it just came out of his and Shaggy's childhood love of Kung Fu movies. A whole lot of their aesthetics are based off things they were into as kids— wrestling, the macabre, the occult, and Faygo soda, to list a few. Since they found success at a young age, they didn't need to give up a lot of their childhood obsessions.

If there's anything about Juggalos only other Juggalos could love, it's their fashion. They dress almost exclusively in ICP's clothing line, Hatchet Gear, which consists of baseball and basketball jerseys, and t-shirts in a hip hop style that's still stuck in the early '90s, with overly baggy pants, sometimes but not always sagging. Though, instead of the usual sports team logos popular to hip hop, they are emblazoned with macabre, leering clowns and ghostly cloaked figures. Around their necks they often wear a gaudy Hatchetman amulet in a bling style on an oversized, diecast chain. It's hard to find a Juggalo who isn't wearing a Psychopathic logo. If they aren't wearing up to three items of Hatchet Gear, they probably at the very least have a couple of tattoos.

Juggalettes often wear the same style as the boys as far as the baggy clothes, but more often they let it all hang out, wearing next to nothing. Less common are the Juggalettes in bright colors with fluorescent hair extensions, platform boots, and glow sticks around their necks—a look resembling ravers or club kids. This is a controversial look and the 'lettes who dress like this tell me they take some shit for looking like ravers. I also see a lot of those baggy pants with all the zippers and chains and straps hanging off them. Teenagers usually sport this style, not older Juggalos. To complement their clothes, Juggalos style their hair in a wide array of alternative fashions, from cornrows like the kind Coolio rocked in the '90s, to mohawks and dyed hair—brightly colored in greens, blues, or purples. Goatees are also common. To the non-Juggalo, it's a bad mashup of appropriated hip hop fashion and the sort of white, alternative fashion commodified by Hot Topic. As an outsider I find it loud and tasteless, but I have to respect their commitment to it. They have an aesthetic that represents them and they *own* it.

Juggalos range widely in ages, and although most of them are teenagers or in their early 20s, we see a lot of Juggalos who are in their 30s or 40s, and even older.

I'd estimate at least a quarter to a third of the Juggalos are women. Most of them prefer the title Juggalette, yet some demand to be called Juggalos. ICP claims the term Juggalette was coined because of an angry feminist somewhere who complained about the lack of a term for women, but they think both genders have a right to the term Juggalo. The idea of feminists forcing a group to apply the suffix "-ette" to anything sounds absurd, as to my knowledge feminists have almost succeeded in putting an end to the condescending suffix altogether. Nonetheless, when Googling "Juggalo + feminist," most of what comes up are angry female Juggalos who reject the term Juggalette and are upset ICP felt coerced into using the term. Juggalo/Juggalette controversy aside, there is little representation of women's voices here; a whole lot of the entertainment at The Gathering is based around their objectification. Faygo wet t-shirt contests. Oil wrestling. Things of that nature. As a matter of fact, degrading women seems to be the rule, and no one of any gender seems to have a problem with it.

One myth of the Juggalo quickly dispelled by our time at The Gathering is the idea that all Juggalos are white. While I didn't completely buy into this assumption, the percentage of people of color at The Gathering surprises me. It seems at least 20% of those attending are made up of African-Americans, Latinos, and Native Americans, proving the Juggalo Family extends beyond the white trash and suburbanite stereotype. In contrast to any other subcultures I've experienced, the Family is far and away the most diverse. Maybe it's my own prejudice and preconceptions about people of color, but I figured mostly white people were attracted to the Family because poor, white folks don't have the same identity politics that one often finds in communities of people of color or queer people. I can see poor, white folks being more desperate for a community like the Juggalo Family because they lack a unified identity based around their oppression. So I feel some shock at seeing Black people wearing the clown makeup and I'm forced to look at the stereotypes I've bought into. For instance, that it's only a logical progression for poor, white folks to put on clown makeup and shout "Whoop! Whoop!," while Black people are stylish and arbiters of what's cool.

Alternative and hipster types have recently targeted the Juggalos as an outlet for their displaced class prejudice. The scapegoating of the Juggalos is another way for the wealthy to play-up stereotypes of the poor and minorities. I don't realize while at The Gathering, but a photographer from one of Seattle's alternative weekly papers also came out to cover the story. She's photographed the Juggalos in my town for a while now, catching them outside ICP shows and posing them in front of dumpsters overflowing with garbage. Seattle, being a wealthy city, yucked it up over these photos and the paper's web page scrolled down endlessly with dehumanizing comments. The hatred Juggalo culture gets is integral to its growth and strength. However, the reporter only stays out here two days, photographing late at night, after the sun goes down on the 105-degree days, and the 'los are well-lit and partying hard during the only four days a year that they get to spend with their Family. She photographs them topless, covered in mud, and standing in front of porta-potties with clown makeup smeared and in disarray, capturing them bleary-eyed, clutching bags of Ecstasy and giant buds of weed.

Whether or not photographing the Juggalos in this manner is exploitative is arguable, seeing as the wasted Juggalos posed for these photographs, but I am shocked at how one-sided they appear. The photos don't show Juggalos grilling and sharing food, or waiting in line for the nasty showers, nor do they show tender Juggalo lovers or, hell, just Juggalos chilling out together simply having a good time. She covers the Juggalos here like she always covers them, from a detached standpoint of bourgeoisie bohemian schadenfreude. It makes me sick to see a young, probably well-educated (I guess I stereotype, too), hip photojournalist come this far to portray the Juggalos in such a way without even the slightest interest in understanding why it's happening. She brags online about how her crew doesn't blend in with their Slayer t-shirts and how she fears getting her camera stolen, implying courage, yet it seems to me she barely dips a toe into the Gathering or Juggalo culture.

Another inaccuracy in her photo series brings me back to the event's ethnicity. In the 46-piece photo series, she only captures five visible people of color. It feels subconsciously intentional. I don't know the photographer's background or story, but in these "postracial" times, the privileged continue to find sneaky ways to lash out at the underclass and reinforce stereotypes. The mainstreaming of Juggalo mockery can be interpreted as a slippery way of laughing at poverty in a way that distances the hip from their own smug elitism—a way of saying, "Look, I'm into cool shit and they're painting themselves up in clown faces and listening to horrible music."

The people of color represented in the photos are dressed more conservatively, in common street clothes with less face paint and Hatchet Gear. Two of the five are Black male performers on stage dressed in hip hop attire, possibly not even Wicked Shit rappers, but simply an act booked for The Gathering. Maybe the white hipster's denial of Black people's involvement in the Juggalo Family illuminates a tokenism they'd rather not admit. Maybe it shows they'd prefer to see Black people as entertainers. Perhaps, they've othered Black people for so long, or fetishized their struggle, that they are reluctant to put in them in a position where they might have to judge them as harshly as white people. Maybe the alternative; leisure class prefers to continue the stereotype that white people have no excuse for being poor, uneducated, and trashy, and are therefore worthy of being mocked and laughed at for their position. In the end, the series of photographs reveals the familiar face of race and class oppression, but now the leisure class doesn't even have to poke fun at white trash to poke fun at white trash. Now they have the Juggalos.

# FLOOBS AND SCRUBS

*I was born, first, they threw me in a shit pile,*

*I dealt with it, and lived there for a while,*

*I got dissed on, pissed on, and beat down,*

*Mutilated, and tossed out a dead clown,*

*Next thing ya know, I'm chillin' at the big top,*

*Free money, and mad bitches non-stop,*

*No water, it's Faygo on tap*

– Violent J, "Pass Me By"

"The only other thing I remember about my real dad, Rick, was him throwing a TV set at my mom. She was standing at the bottom of the stairs, and he was at the top. She had to pull me out of the way as it came crashing down," recounts Violent J of one of his earliest memories from the age of two. Afterwards, his father took off, swiping his and J's mom's savings from her hand, never to be seen again.

This began Joe Bruce's (aka Violent J) childhood with his brother, Rob Bruce, and their sister, Theresa. From then on, a revolving door of seemingly sociopathic stepfathers and boyfriends who humiliated, degraded, and physically abused them, and even kicked their dog around, entered their lives. He tells these stories in his autobiography, *ICP: Behind the Paint*, in a laidback way, but the wounds are still raw.

He also tells a story about a horrible babysitter who locked them in an empty backyard on the days their mother worked. They cherished moments when the neighbor dog dug through the fence to play with them. At times, the babysitter's own kids came into the backyard. "I hated playing with them. See, they had this fucked-up habit of unzipping their pants and waggling their dicks at us, then chasing us around like that." J's mother knew they were unhappy; he says, "If we complained... all she'd say was 'there's nothing I can do about it; I don't know who else to get.' She was telling the truth; there really was nobody else." The level of desperation in this statement illuminates the hardship this single-mother family of four went through.

As kids who experienced hell at home, they often got little relief in school where the Bruce brothers were "legendary scrubs." They were often in debt to their school, owing lunch money, and their names were announced over the PA, letting everyone know they couldn't pay. "If you step on a cracked tile, you gotta kiss one of the Bruce brothers," girls would say around school.

The Juggalos respect Violent J's rough childhood because the Juggalos are outcasts too. I guess that's where I come in. I feel compassion for the Juggalos because I was an outcast at school, too. I never owned the right clothes in middle and high school, my family struggled financially, and there was a lot of shit going on at home. More importantly, my family had just taken a serious dive. We moved from being a middle-class family in Bismarck, North Dakota to a financially struggling family in a rough, white, working class town right outside of Gary, Indiana. To make it worse, I had been homeschooled for years by my Pentecostal mother, my only outside exposures being a church youth group and other weird, freak, homeschool kids. When we moved to Indiana, I was thrown into a violent junior high in the middle of the school year. I had no idea how things worked, no social skills, weighed about 80 pounds, and was years away from puberty. I had so little world experience that if kids asked me if I was jacking off, I honestly didn't know. I was fucked. I sat completely alone in the cafeteria every day. I'm not saying this to piggy-back, or in any way say I had it as bad as Violent J, but to state why I feel for the Juggalos. I know how important it is to find a place where you fit—I'm still trying to do it. It's also probably why I root for the underdog. Charles Baudelaire once said, "Genius is nothing more nor less than childhood recaptured at will." And if anybody's nailed that action, it's Violent J. He epitomizes escape, a tactic that not only saved him as a child, but is a cornerstone of Psychopathic Records' empire and the core of his own success. By escape, I mean the obsessions that he, his brother, and later Joe Ulster (who would become Shaggy 2

Dope) used to escape the real world and to cope, obsessions that became keys to their success.

Some of these obsessions include:

1. Wrestling and ninja movies. They were so obsessed with these genres they started their own backyard wrestling leagues as teenagers. *Kung Fu Theater* influenced them to start calling each other "ninja." Both these childhood consequences stuck with them into adulthood, up to the point where they wrestled as Insane Clown Posse in major federations and eventually started their own Juggalo Class Wrestling.

2. Hip hop. Violent J and Shaggy discovered rap early in their preteens. They started hip hop crews inspired by Run-DMC and UTFO and even went through phases of graffiti and breakdancing.

3. The Supernatural. Violent J strongly believes he is in tune to spiritual worlds and has never faltered in this belief. It started when he and his brother saw God. According to a story in his biography, their mom went out of town for a week and left them $50 for food, and they were stoked to spend it all on stuff like chips and dip and pizza. But the neighborhood bully found out about it and intimidated them into letting him stay the night; he ate all their chips and dip and ruined everything. That is, until J and Rob saw God. Both of them saw a black hooded figure coming up the stairs and they knew it was God showing them everything was going to be okay, in spite of the bully fucking up their night. It's my favorite part of Violent J's book, because even as an adult it has this tone of "ha ha, the mean ol' bully didn't get to see God coming up the stairs." He continued to have

these supernatural experiences, eventually leading to the Dark Carnival.

4. Floob Pride. Another thing they carried over from the pain of their childhood was the concept of being a "floob" or a "scrub." Violent J and Rob owned this, said "fuck it!" and began taking pride in being poor and trashy. They proudly rode their shitty Huffys while other kids rode Diamondbacks and Mongooses, and even asked their mother to pull right up in front of the school to drop them off in her beat-up hooptie. They said "fuck it" to school and education. They slacked off and wrestled and did petty crime instead. Violent J tells these stories with as much conviction as Malcolm X tells of his education and enlightenment. And why not? It's his story. It worked for him. Whatever the Juggalos have gone through or might be going through, Violent J suffered something similar. When Violent J grew up, he threw them into the Juggalo mix. The Juggalos were the kids that didn't fit in. They were the fat kids, the ugly kids, and the poor kids. Proud floobs! Juggalos!

# THESE ISLANDS

*If I only could, I'd set the world on fire. Say,* Fuck the world!
Fuck the world!

— Insane Clown Posse, "Fuck the World"

 middle-aged Juggalo, shirtless and tattooed in
Psychopathic designs, tells me the heat index is up
to 110 degrees. It's still morning.

"Stay hydrated," he says.

The sweltering temperature is supposed to continue for
the rest of The Gathering—heavy, sticky heat that makes one
want to just lay around all day. The sun shines bright and high
overhead, and there's no shade to be found.

It forces me and Damon to hit up a small, manmade
lake, like one you might find at some crappy summer camp,
affectionately called Hepatitis Lake. It's not bad, despite its
foreboding nickname, brackish green tint, and all the trash

floating around in it. (It was chemically treated for the event.) The water isn't as cool as I want, but it still offers a break from the brutal heat. Juggalos bob up and down in the water or dig their feet deep down in the mud outside the shallow-end barricade. Sitting out on the dock are about 25 Juggalos and maybe three Juggalettes. Besides engaging in the age-old activity of shoving your buddy in the water when he's not paying attention, they're having a lot of fun fucking around with the balance of the dock. Too many of them stand at one corner of the dock, then the side opposite rises up several feet and a whole passel of flaily-limbed skinny Juggalos and fat, tattooed, hairy ones, tumble off into the lake, laughing and cursing. There's something endlessly comic about it that keeps me watching and waiting for it to happen again.

Thin Juggalos buoy on their big girlfriends, arms wrapped around each other as they make out, then tease and splash other friends in their small group. After years of only knowing the Juggalos from their video blogs, poorly-spelled message board postings, and angry, defensive retorts to haters via YouTube comments, I'm warmed by the adorableness in these young misfits. Everybody is completely stoked to be out here. For the Juggalos, this is Shangri-La on earth, a small piece of heaven before returning to lives that are at best banal, but more likely oppressive and hard. They laugh! They freestyle! They drink Faygo! They throw shit! It's still morning and the heat already starts to break down me and Damon. But give the Juggalos a bit of shade or a lake and they won't stop the party. They scraped, saved, hustled, borrowed, and stole every cent they could to get here, and now they're ready to live it up.

My mind slips back to the beginning of my trip to The Gathering three weeks ago: drunk as piss and buying the plane ticket online. It was a crossing of the Rubicon for me. The Gathering slid right up next to a festival I attend every year. That same night I packed to head out to the woods for two weeks with my friends. I didn't plan ahead for The Gathering. I knew I was going, but due to my own self-doubt I put off planning for it until the last minute and came out ill-prepared. I guess, like the Juggalos, I'm a bit of a floob. I fuck things up. I lack confidence and come from a place where everyone pretty much told me I was bound to fail.

Days after I bought my ticket, a group of my friends and I lay under blankets in a meadow, under a broad belly of stars, miles from any civilization in a Northern California forest. We dropped E and huddled together close while the temperature of our bodies dropped with the night air. We laughed that night long into the morning, then watched the sun rise, waking amorous color around us. I refused to talk of this undertaking of The Gathering to my friends, but I needed the support of my people more than anything at that moment.

There's something to be said for completely stripping your guard down—having these moments go on for a few days or a couple weeks are enough to shed the city for a while. We strip ourselves of all outside worries, of all the condescending eyes, all the traffic and debt and newscasts of war and entropy. Hopefully we mentally stay in that place for a good long time, with at least a few days to let our true selves emerge from our layers of armor—armor that's so much a part of us we can't remember strapping some of it on. We stop thinking twice about what we say and do and bullshit perceptions. For a few days, we slip out of the judgmental eyes of the world, and spend them laughing and romping and getting fucked-up or doing whatever the hell it is we do with our friends, whatever it was that brought us together in the first place. We just feel... home. This is the reason people do seemingly cheesy things like Burning Man, or a science fiction con, or whatever it might be. One may grow weary of some of the bullshit elements of the event or the actions of some of the other folks that show up and fuck things up, but the tightness with people that actually "get it," the feeling of solidarity, leaves an imprint. As humans we need these zones, these islands. Fuck the world!

And Juggalos probably hate hippies as much as I do.

·        ·        ·

"*Blam!*" goes an M-80 thrown by a Juggalo on the other side of Hepatitis Lake, blowing a hole in the side of someone's tent. Juggalos on the dock start shouting, "*You fucked up! You fucked up!*" at the 'lo who set it off. The complete lack of security gives The Gathering a weird *Lord of the Flies* feel. When someone does something that goes against what the majority of Juggalos deem appropriate, the "*You fucked up!*" chant will go up. If enough of them are displeased, some action takes place. I've heard tell of a thing called a Juggalo Jury where a Juggalo is tried by a court of their peers and, if found guilty, receives some form of punishment for their wrongdoing. So for instance, if a Juggalo stole from another, he doesn't get thrown out of The Gathering by a bunch of security goons, he just serves out his sentence.

This is a good example of the sympathy Juggalos show each other. One of the penances is doing time in Juggalo Jail—a small, round, red and yellow barred structure resembling something that might be found on top of playground equipment. A convicted Juggalo can even watch the acts from their cell, as it's located right in front of the stage. It's all in good fun. Juggalos fuck up sometimes, but they keep each other in check. They also use the "*Fam-uh-lee*" chant to regulate The Gathering. It gets the 'los to come to their senses; they're all here for Clown Love and the "*Fam-uh-lee*" chant reminds them of that. It's used to stop fights and stop people from representing the Family poorly. This (as of yet) benign ochlocracy keeps The Gathering from utter chaos. There are 20,000 people here, for God's sake. ICP puts a lot of faith in the Juggalo Family to keep things in order this way; they have a lot banked on it.

•　　•　　•

The first people we make buddies with are Jared and Mark. In the field acting as a parking lot where we're all camped, we are laughing at some hothead attendant—a hired local who just chewed us out over how we parked and set up camp. Nothing like bonding over some random asshole to break the ice between strangers. Jared is a white dude in his mid-30s from Lansing, Michigan. He wears a Michigan sports team t-shirt and shorts. He's here with his stepbrother, Mark, who is also a nice enough fellow, but too stoned-out-of-his-gourd to articulate most of the time. It's their first Gathering, too.

"Are you a Juggalo?" I ask Jared.

"Well… " he pauses. "Yeah, I guess," answering with an awkward smile.

I'm not sure why he's reluctant to say he's a Juggalo. Perhaps he doesn't feel like he's down enough to quite take on the title, or really doesn't feel like one and feels put on the spot. The question itself, though, is out of the ordinary here. And I'm glad, for my own safety, that I posed it to him first. Of course he's a Juggalo—this is the Gathering of the Juggalos.

"Are you?" he asks, going along with how I kicked off the conversation.

"No," I say, "I just like rap. And I'm a writer, so I figured I'd come out here to check it out."

I continue to use this as my excuse for being at The Gathering, if I choose to out myself. Though sometimes I think it best to leave out the "writer" part. After a while, Damon comes over and I introduce him. Jared sits in his car playing hip hop and rolling blunts while chatting it up with us.

"Yeah," he turns to me after a while and says, more confidently, "I'm a Juggalo. I got into them back in '95 with their *Ringmaster* album. I was a really big fan when they were just coming up, but I wasn't into where they were going with their later stuff. Now I'm going back and catching up on some the stuff I've missed."

He pulls down his sock to show us his right calf tattooed with the *Ringmaster* logo.

"It's actually backwards," he says with a smile. "The tattoo artist fucked up and put the transfer on backwards. I just say you're supposed to look at it in the mirror."

# DARK CARNIVAL

*It's a full moon and the riddles are calling,*

*Three more cards and the skies will be falling,*

*But don't take it from me, I'm just a clown,*

*Wicked clown, wicked town,*

*Juggalugagaluga lick it down*

> – Insane Clown Posse, "The Show Must Go On"

*Because of my vision, and what happened over the next couple of days, I began to realize that I either was chosen for a grand purpose in this world, or I had gone completely insane.*

> – Violent J, *ICP: Behind the Paint*

In the early '90s, ICP stood for Inner City Posse—a gangsta rap group made up of Violent J, Shaggy 2 Dope, and Shaggy's brother, John Utsler, who performed as John Kickjazz. There was some verisimilitude to their criminal-minded lyrics, as they lived like street thugs; except they weren't actually a gang. Nonetheless, their first release, an EP titled *Dog Beats*, became a regional hit and they started getting threats from actual gangs in the Detroit area. They changed their name to distance themselves from their gangsta themes and avoid the beef they were getting. They also felt they should represent Detroit more by not playing the same kind of rap LA was exporting at the time with groups like NWA. They took some notes from Esham, (a Detroit rapper who used Satanic imagery, extreme violence, and a macabre horror movie tone in his songs as allegory) to illuminate issues people in the ghetto struggled with. With song titles like "Red Rum" and "KKKill The Fetus," Esham called his music "acid rap," and strongly influenced what would soon be known as horrorcore (so much that he is often credited with being the inventor of the genre). ICP wanted to get on the horrorcore tip, but wanted to put their own twist on it, and thus came up with Wicked Shit. They also wanted to keep the initials ICP so the locals would know they were the same group. At this point, Violent J had his epiphany. According to his autobiography, *ICP: Behind the Paint*, it hit him all at once and he knew he'd figured it out.

Violent J writes, describing his big *a-hah* moment, the one that would make them into the underground stars they are today: "Listen… I got that Detroit shit… our shit is going to have tons of our own humor mixed in, right? *Clowns!* We're scrubby-ass killer clowns. Then it hit me all at once–*boom!* Let's all paint our faces like clowns and be the Insane Clown Posse: clowns who murder and kill people who deserve to be murdered or killed. '*Whoooosh!*'"

Later, on the night of J's epiphany, the Clown revealed itself even further. Violent J went home "excited as fuck about the whole thing," and while still wide awake, he had a vision in which his whole room turned into an eerie carnival.

"The carnival was completely surrounding me on all sides, and was as twisted and strange as fuck. Standing not ten feet away from me was the clown I had seen many times in my dreams, but this time he was all too real as he sat staring back at me. He had white clown makeup on in a strange pattern. He wore a pink jester's hat, and a clown suit with big clown shoes and white gloves. He held in his left hand a deck of giant playing cards. Each one was a joker's card, like you might see in a normal deck of cards."

The clown started dropping the cards on the ground, the whole time talking to him with no words coming out of his mouth. Just before the last card dropped, Violent J found himself high above everything and could see that the carnival was headed to a town. Then blackness...

"Then loud as fuck. All I could hear was screams and the sounds of chaos and people dying and bizarre laughter. It got mega loud as fuck, but I saw nothing," says Violent J.

After he came down from his vision, he says, "I began to realize that either I was chosen for a grand purpose or completely insane." He decided to go with the former and started the Juggalo faith, known as the Dark Carnival. He felt he was called by these "spirit ninjas" to spread the message of the Dark

Carnival on earth, and to lead people on a pure and righteous path. The tenets of the Dark Carnival revealed themselves in the next six ICP albums, called the Joker's Cards. Insane Clown Posse albums teach moral lessons where the wicked are judged for their bad actions and sent to Hell's Pit, while those who lived a morally upright life go to Shangri-La—the Juggalo heaven. This is the wisdom they grace upon the Juggalos through all the gore and violence.

"The strangest thing that happened to me after that vision was that suddenly ideas and images would pop into my head with ease as if there was an energy or beings who where [sic] channeling through me and feeding me this information. It became all too clear to me what my purpose in life was. For me, the Dark Carnival in my vision is something real and something that is coming. Maybe it won't look exactly like it did in my vision, but something out there is coming, and it is going to consume all those souls who are not pure," says Violent J.

They believe the violence in their songs "hold[s] up a mirror that might help some people get on a more righteous path, so they won't spend eternity burning in Hell." Yet Violent J also claims not to "believe all the traditional Bible beliefs as to what is considered a sin."

This is where it all gets very confusing. I've listened to almost every album by ICP during my research, and the message is still lost on me. I have trouble picking up on the morality in the metaphors. To me, the songs just seem like a lot of rap about hacking people up, and some scatological stupidity about stuff like eating Monopoly and shitting-out Connect Four. Sure, I understand the justice in songs about inflicting violence on child molesters, wife beaters, and other "people that deserve it," but those morals contradict with their songs about attacking women, bystanders, and other innocents I have trouble believing "deserve it." Hell, even a dog and a cat get it in some of their songs.

In an interview with Bill O'Reilly where he's questioned about the violence in his lyrics, Violent J says,, "There's a difference between entertainment and reality. I'm sitting here with a painted face."

Art should be gory and violent at times. It should push people's buttons. It should go places that you can't in real life. But what's questionable is how confused ICP's message is. One minute they're saying their music is religious, and the next they're saying it's entertainment. They sing about cartoonish violence a lot, but they also boast about actually beating people up for disrespecting them, too—whether it be a musician who comes backstage to meet them while they're applying makeup (a major offense to ICP), an 18-year-old in a Waffle House in Greenfield, Indiana who talks shit to them, or even a Juggalo who flips them off. Fictional Wicked Clowns in their songs are the dealers of moral justice to evildoers, but these fictional Clowns will be just as guilty in the next song; there's no consistency. But if there's one regularity to ICP, it's how they double down on everything they say with the conviction of a zealot. And by proxy, the Juggalos do too. So many Juggalos I talk to quote verbatim things Violent J and Shaggy have said. I've also heard stories of people who were threatened and attacked for "not respecting ICP". It takes quite a bit of blind faith to get behind the Dark Carnival message, to not walk away from it reeling at its confused message. To get it, you must be a Juggalo. It's a Tilt-

A-Whirl of thought which makes the Juggalos unable to see the hypocrisies and holes in the Dark Carnival faith. It also allows ICP to never take responsibility for their actions.

Violent J continues with the contradictions by saying one doesn't have to wear Hatchet Gear or drink Faygo, and one doesn't even have to like Insane Clown Posse or Psychopathic Records, to be a Juggalo. He says some Juggalos haven't even heard of ICP or even know they're Juggalos— but if one is a Juggalo, the truth of the Dark Carnival will come to them. However, I've yet to see this happen. Every Juggalo I've met buys into the whole package. Personally, if truth comes from a guy in face paint hosing me down with a two-liter of generic soda, I'm fucked for believing it. And I think that's how most people feel. I've yet to meet someone who just casually likes Psychopathic Records. The message just doesn't get over on the eclectic music fan, the merely curious, or the fascinated gawker (such as myself). If it makes any sense at all to you, you buy the whole package. The Juggalo Family is *your* family, Faygo is *your* beverage, Hatchetgear is *your* wardrobe, and *you* are down with the Clown. But then again, maybe that's giving too much credit to ICP. Maybe, if it makes any sense at all to you, you've felt Clown Love.

# FAYGO BEVERAGES, INC

*We was butt naked all over the floor, it felt weird, though,*

*'cause we was at the Faygo store*

— Insane Clown Posse, "$50 Bucks"

Faygo soda is a huge thing with the Juggalos. Insane Clown Posse hoses down the crowd with it at their shows: throwing and drop-kicking countless two-liter bottles into the audience, or spraying it all over them with a fire hose. No raincoats are worn, as the crowd joyfully gets drenched in the sugary stickiness, writhing in it as one solid mass.

Faygo is a generic pop from the Michigan area and comes in 50 different flavors. As kids, ICP loved drinking it. It was cheap, so they had it around their homes. It's a combination of regional pride and working class symbolism. They've always denied any sponsorship from Faygo, claiming it's just a part of the Juggalo mythology.

At first, it's disturbing how much Juggalos are into Faygo. It suggests the influence of ICP is encompassing to the point where they affect the kind of pop the Juggalos drink. But it's actually more innocent and a bit sweeter than that. A Juggalo goes to their first ICP show and gets drenched in Faygo, dancing and moving with a huge crowd, feeling the Clown Love. They feel its stickiness on their skin, taste the sugar on their tongue. They feel like they finally belong somewhere, and Faygo becomes the symbol of that. You could compare it to someone who does their first hit of acid at a Phish show, and Phish becomes a symbol of that awakening forever after.

Faygo and the Dark Carnival's cohesion goes way back to one of ICP's very first shows, when Insane Clown Posse procured a bunch of two-liters of Faygo and set them up on the side of the stage. Violent J says they just wanted the audience to be able to see it sitting there because they rapped about it in their songs. During the set, some kid flipped J off and he got so pissed he just opened one of the bottles and chucked it at the kid. The kid threw it back, and suddenly the crowd grabbed the rest of the bottles and started spraying them everywhere. The soda has been part of the ICP legend ever since.

·　　　·　　　·

At 1:45 in a tent called the Bomb House, Ron Jeremy—the porn star famous for his enormous dong—still hasn't shown up to host the wet t-shirt contest where a bunch of Juggalettes will be hosed down with Faygo. I showed up 20 minutes late myself and I'm still waiting. A whole lot of restless 'los and, considering the entertainment, a significant amount of 'lettes pack into the circus-sized tent. There are up to 800 bodies inside the tent, kicking the heat up to 115 or 120 degrees. Suddenly the crowd splits, like when the circle opens in a mosh pit, dividing the front and back of the crowd who've both armed themselves with beer cans and Faygo bottles and whatever else was around.

The front half shouts, *"Fuck the back! Fuck the back!"*

The rear calls out in response, *"Fuck the front! Fuck the front!"*

And trash just flies and flies. My position in the middle isn't safe, as bottles are winged joyfully in every direction. Bottles, cans, wadded-up paper plates, and empty balloons that no longer contain nitrous fly from one side to another. As I try to take some photos of the battle, I get pegged in the head with a beer can from behind. I turn to a short, skinny 'lo with white-boy cornrows about 10 yards away and half-hidden in the crowd. He throws up his hands in the universal sign of "I dunno," hamming it up with a mischievous grin,. I flip him the bird with a smile. He appreciates it. Then the crowd moves about and obscures him completely.

Ron Jeremy still hasn't arrived and there's no sign of the wet t-shirt girls. The Juggalos grow weary of trash-fighting, but still they wait. The tent is insufferably hot and the crowd noticeably thins out, but a lot remain.

Ron Jeremy shows up about 45 minutes late. He's pelted with trash and booed by the crowd.

*"You fucked up! You fucked up!"* the restless, overheated crowd chants at Jeremy.

Eventually, they settle down long enough for Jeremy to drag some 'lettes on the stage.

About eight barely-legal girls shake their asses, getting sprayed down with bottles of Faygo from 'los in the crowd. The t-shirts are pretty much non-existent, and it doesn't take long for the bikini tops to come off as well. Jeremy encourages them to get into some girl-on-girl action. The winner will receive a grip of Psychopathic Records merch, and they're working hard for it. But they're having too much fun to be motivated only by that; these girls love to perform. A couple of the girls on the stage are pretty heavy. Juggalo body/beauty standards differ from mainstream society—a Juggalette is a Juggalette, and thus hot for being a Juggalette. Fat girls can get mad respect in the Dark Carnival. They get up and grind the pole with the skinny 'lettes, and the 'los are stoked.

Feeling like I've had enough and nauseated from the heat, I work my way to the rear of the tent. There I see a shirtless 'lo who looks to be in his late 20s. He sports a tattoo of the Batman logo with the word "Twiztid", a Psychopathic Records band, in place of the superhero's name. He kneels and a child of about five pours blue Faygo soda over him.

I walk in a heat-induced fog back to the van. The miserable weather does nothing but intensify how out of place I feel. I cut through the Midway, past the corndogs, the elephant ears, the Fat Ass Chop and Jumbo Bitch Beaters. Already sun sick and irritable, I find myself judging the Juggalos harshly, maybe the harshest I ever have. Sure, they have fashion and aesthetics only a Juggalo could love, but right now I'm genuinely grossed-out by the ubiquity of Hatchet Gear merchandising, the way it hangs so loose and oversized off the Juggalos bodies. I have to acknowledge just how unhealthy the Juggalos look to me—

skinny and pale or flabby and obese. I watch them lounging and munching elephant ears or Jumbo Bitch Beaters, hopefully in the shade if they can manage to find some. I'm judging people on their bodies, what they're eating. It's a lot easier to be body positive in the punk and DIY communities I'm used to. It's easier to be open-minded in a culture where someone who is a bit husky is eating greens from their garden or cooking dumpstered produce rather than munching on corn dogs and swigging Faygo on a carnival midway. I don't like these thoughts I'm having, so cruel and elitist. It reminds me of my job driving a taxi and working the poorer areas of town, driving folks back from the grocery store and unloading their groceries: everything pre-packaged and all junk food, with few vegetables or fruit. I'm forced to confront how I feel out here. On the surface it's so completely foreign, but it also carries with it an uncomfortable familiarity to places I've long left behind, never wanting to revisit. After years of defending the Juggalos and virtuously arguing that they're oppressed, not because they're Juggalos but because of their class, I'm forced to summon the courage of these convictions.

I wonder how my radical West Coast friends would act out here. Would they judge everything they see, without considering why and how it's happening? Probably. What would my feminist friends think of the entertainment being wet t-shirt contests and oil wrestling and songs about bitches? Offended, of course. The Juggalos are judged constantly, but few outsiders have gotten down with them to see what they are all about. Then there's me. Me and my self-described pro-sleaze buddy... and whatever I choose to leave out of the tale. But right now, I'm just kind of sickened by everything, not to mention heat-sick in the sweltering humidity.

·        ·        ·

I walk past the wide, sprawling Psychopathic Records/Hatchet Gear merch booth, which provides plenty of shade and items for ICP's working class and struggling "floob" fanbase to purchase. I walk past the autograph tent, which eventually provides shade if one waits long enough in the snaking line to get inside. Outside, Juggalos wait endlessly in the blazing sun, sweating and sunburnt, to get their stuff signed by their favorite Psychopathic Records artists. I wonder how much I could hock Violent J's autobiography for if I get it signed, but the line is very, very long.

ICP constantly boasts about their success and how the Juggalos aided in that success. Even though they're the "most hated band in the world," ICP sells tons and tons of CDs, stickers, hats, ball jerseys and shorts, diecast Hatchetman necklaces, Bobblehead dolls, action figures and comics, and more because of the rabid commitment of their followers. They'll make different versions of an album so they can sell multiple copies. They gloat over how many CD's they sell as physical media dies. They take pride in the loyalty of their followers. So fuck the mainstream, fuck the music industry, they say. They got theirs.

"They lose thousands of dollars on The Gathering every year. They just do it to give something back to us," Juggalos tell me.

And the Juggalos appreciate this selfless act.

Violent J and Shaggy may tell us how to get to Shangri-La, but as far as telling us how to live until then, well... it looks like we're on our own. The point of Wicked Shit doesn't seem to be encouraging the elevation of their followers. Violent J is no Chuck D, pushing his fans to educate themselves and to rise above. It's clear the highest good of Juggalo culture is to simply be a Juggalo.

But I'm forgetting the Dark Carnival, and how God called on ICP to lead the Juggalos out of Hell's Pit to Shangri-La. Who needs knowledge when someone pimps the Ultimate Truth? Especially while doing it through fresh rap songs?

"You have to respect ICP" is something I hear Juggalos say all the time out here. But as much as I try to see where Juggalos come from on this, I can't respect ICP. Maybe I'm too much of a set-in-my-ways radical, but I'm only able to see them as power hungry, poverty profiteers. And this makes me a hater.

# SHANGRI-LA AND DARK CARNIVAL DEFINED

*The truth is we follow God*

*We've always been behind Him*

*the Carnival is God and may all Juggalos find Him...*

*May the Juggalos find God*

*We're not sorry that we tricked you*

*the Carnival will carry on*

*Suck my nuts, bitch, fuck you...*

        – Insane Clown Posse, "Thy Unveiling"

The Love Wagon drives by slowly.

    *"Fuck your walkin'! Fuck your walkin'! Fuck your walkin'!"* Juggalos chant from the wagon.

I grab some of the ever-present trash on the ground and whip it at the young 'los.

"Let's get on!" Damon shouts and starts limp-jogging, his left leg stiff.

We climb on The Love Wagon, despite the rule we're not supposed to when it's moving. Like all the rules at The Gathering, it's just there to be broken. It's mostly a younger group of 'los on the hard, wooden wagon and it's complete chaos, except for the unison of their chanting.

The wagon turns a corner, passing the Bomb House. There, a 'lo and a 'lette set up a table with probably around 50 assorted sizes and colors of plastic bottles filled with water, all for the sole purpose of chucking them at The Love Wagon. Damon and I duck and cover our heads as The Love Wagon riders take this barrage like soldiers, the young 'los smiling and flipping-off the offense and throwing back the bottles.

The Love Wagon continues on as the Juggalos chant in unison.

"*Fuck your walkin'!*" they chant to 'los walking.

"*Fuck your campin'!*" they chant to 'los camping.

"*Fuck your corn dog!*" they chant to a guy with a corn dog.

And, of course, the wild, primal call of "*Show your tits!*" when there are… tits.

"*That smells good! That smells good! That smells good!*" they chant to a grill full of wieners.

"*Old school titties! Old school titties! Old school titties!*" they chant as we pass a completely naked 60-year-old displaced hippie and her fully clothed partner.

When we round the curve, the second stage comes into view. A huge flank of 'los and 'lettes emerge from behind a staggered row of tents and bombard us with countless water balloons—the scene comparable to one of those old medieval movies where a phalanx of archers shoot a ton of arrows all at once, blackening the sky. We're getting soaked and laughing hysterically at The Love Wagon's honorable defeat. Then we jump off The Love Wagon and get down to business.

"*Titties! Titties!*" We hear as it fades into the distance.

What was the question I was set to ask? Oh yeah…What is Shangri-La? I take out the tape recorder and start asking questions.

"Shangri-La and what it means to me is all about Karma, you know," a Juggalo named Jason, 21, tells us. "Violent J… He wanted to show two different afterlives and, personally, I really don't believe in an afterlife. But Shangri-La is, like, a paradise where you can be at Hakuna Matata, a good state of mind. No worries. You know, you're just there, kickin' it. You've got Hell's Pit and you've got Shangri-La and you didn't want any of the Juggalos to go to Hell's Pit, 'cause if you listen to the CDs, Shangri-La is all about the Juggalos…all about the Juggalos. And then Hell's Pit's just all dark and evil."

Many Juggalos repeat this "just kickin' [it]" phrase or say "just chillin'" when they talk of what Shangri-La means to them. Some of them believe it's something in the future. Others, like Jason, believe it's in the present. But they all see Shangri-La as a place of respite and peace—a place where they can be themselves in a world where they feel like outcasts.

"I believe that this world will end. It will be destroyed, taking all the people who aren't followers of the Dark Carnival," Bloodrain says as he sips on my whiskey bottle. "Then a new world will be made here which will be Shangri-La for Juggalos."

I ask him about good people who aren't Juggalos, if they'll be saved and allowed entry into this post-earth afterlife. I feel that he thinks I'm referring to myself, but I'm actually referring to someone more like… his grandma, who I'm assuming isn't a Juggalo. Coming from a Pentecostal background, I know full well the weight of having all the truth. Knowing family and friends are headed toward eternal damnation for being non-believers can take a heavy toll on the believer.

"Yeah, if they're good people they'll make it, too," Bloodrain says, and points a thumb to his buddy, "Can he get a drink?"

"Sure," I say and he passes it.

His painted-up friend takes a humble swig and hands it back to me.

The "good people" clause may refer to what Violent J is saying about how Juggalos exist who don't rock the Hatchet Gear and have never heard of ICP, and even some Juggalos who don't even know they're Juggalos. I've heard several Juggalos repeat this saying; they know Juggalos who have never heard of ICP. I think what they're getting at is that there's some kind of Shangri-La pass for ninjas, like your family and friends who don't willingly participate in the Dark Carnival. Nevertheless, a lot of Juggalos I talk to find Bloodrain's apocalyptic take on Shangri-La controversial. They think he's a little out there, and they don't like the implied judgment day. Despite Violent J's hell and damnation tenets, most Juggalos are more flippant about it all and shrug off the afterlife aspect of it altogether.

"It's a big-ass stepping stone," says Topher, a chubby, warm-hearted Juggalo from Cincinnati. "It's just like the dude who said we're all gonna take over the world, blah-di-blah-blah... I really don't think that's what needs to happen, I just think it's a whole mentality of freedom... Once everyone feels like they're free, then they are. You don't feel free, you're not free. That's what freedom's about."

"I don't see it only as an afterlife," says Dom from Milwaukee. "This (The Gathering) is Shangri-La because it's the happiest place on earth. This could be Shangri-La. Heaven could be Shangri-La. Whatever keeps 'em out of my face could be Shangri-La."

On a sensational level, it's disappointing that the Juggalos' Dark Carnival comes across as so simple to them. That despite the Judeo-Christian overtones, Shangri-La means just kickin' it with your homies at a place like The Gathering, or "just people taking care of each other, like it should be," as another 'lo told me. But it is heartening that the Dark Carnival and the Juggalo Family stem from a basic human need. To most Juggalos the two are one and the same. They come to this understanding when they see an ICP show or attend the Gathering, and realize their faith and the Family are intertwined.

"We're fuckin' in Shangri-La right now. Juggalo Island all day," Jame-o from Atlanta tells me. "This is what I fell into. I fell into something and finally felt like something accepted me. You know what I mean? I can't imagine heaven being much better."

"If you see anybody that's too fucked up, please, get them some water and let them live," he adds.

•       •       •

Insane Clown Posse disappointed a lot of Juggalos when they released the 6th and final Joker's Card album, *The Wraith*. The highly-anticipated album dropped the final message of the Dark Carnival in the song "Thy Unveiling," which starts with the sound of a thunderstorm and builds with a deep and ominous tension, listing off the previous five Joker's Cards: *Carnival of Carnage*, *The Ringmaster*, *The Riddlebox*, *The Great Milenko*, and *The Amazing Jeckel Brothers*.

"Looks like we're all out of time, brother," Violent J says. "Everybody's out of time. Fuck it, we gots to tell 'em… "

They go on to tell the Juggalos that "the Dark Carnival is God, not sorry that we tricked you. May the Juggalos find God."

This caused quite a stir amongst the Juggalos. Some of them felt betrayed and fooled into Christianity. Many converted, and others adapted their own personal philosophies and spirituality to fit into this final message. From my understanding though, few Juggalos felt upset enough to up and leave their Family.

Sid, a transgender African-American Juggalo from Ohio, tells me he was raised in a rigid and oppressive Pentecostal family. He sees the Dark Carnival as a way to reconnect with his spirituality, without all the fear and hate that surrounded his upbringing. It makes things simpler. He says,

Shangri-La to me is, basically... it's like heaven for people who are good people. You don't have to be a Juggalo to go to Shangri-La. For me it seems like I can just be a good person and do good things and go there. The whole thing that pissed me off about Christianity is, you know, I mean there's Christians who want to go to Shangri-La obviously, but I'm just saying, how they think about Heaven, it's like you gotta do all this perfect shit. If you're not perfect you're not gonna make it. Like if you don't speak in tongues, if you don't do this, this, this, this, and this then you're fuckin' not gonna make it. And it's just like, there are really good people out there who are not in heaven—to their standards—because they're not speaking a certain language? That doesn't make any sense. So for Shangri-La, you can do, you know, whatever, just be a good fuckin' person, help out people every once in a while, or something and you're gonna go up there, you know. It's just another version of heaven for people who aren't accepted.

Sid isn't the only Juggalo who takes some of the biblical message of the Dark Carnival literally. Bubbles, a thin, female Juggalo with long dreads and hair laced and lit with countless glow sticks, and a wearing puffy Day-Glo dress, explains, "Shangri-La really is a paradise to me, whenever your day comes, whenever the reaper is knocking on your door, The Wraith has like, as I like to call it, he's gonna set you straight. If you steal, and you hate, and you have prejudice, all those things that cause horrible, horrible things, you will go to Hell's Pit, and you will sit there with the demon and burn forever. And the afterlife, like, if you use your karma and you do your shit straight, you'll end up in Shangri-La. Sippin' on a Faygo and smokin' a blunt all day long."

The fluidity of each Juggalo's interpretation of the Joker's Cards interests me. Unlike Christianity, it appears every Juggalo respects his fellow 'los' take on the Cards. No one claims a monopoly on spiritual truth, and even though some of them, like Bubbles, might literally believe in Hell's Pit, they don't come across as high 'n' mighty enough to tell anyone they're going there. Instead, they look at the Six Cards as warnings against immoral action in their own lives. Unlike the Christian beliefs the Dark Carnival is rooted in, it's up to the individual 'lo to work out their own salvation. How a 'lo chooses to view the Cards is respected as the truth for them. Juggalos don't argue each other's personal doctrine.

Maybe this is what they're referring to when they talk about "Juggalos who don't even know they're Juggalos." Maybe they're talking about people whom they see as living a righteous life, regardless of affiliation or being down with the Clown. And while the Juggalos have many words for a fake Juggalo—a Juffalo or a Juggahoe—they generally don't damn the non-Juggalos. Not to say that Juggalos don't harbor some resentment for the rest of the world at times, but it seems to be based more around defensiveness than spiritual elitism.

"They gave us some shit for it, but whatever, I like it," Neil from Massachusetts says to me when asked about the "Miracles" video.

Neil is one of the rare Juggalos I speak to who even knows how high the level of mockery of the "Miracles" video reached. Most Juggalos I meet who are aware of the mocking are pretty flippant about it, though some can get defensive. Juggalos are used to getting crap for following the "most hated band in the world," and don't expect those outside of the Dark Carnival to understand.

"I love the 'Miracles' video," a Juggalo named Fuckstick relays. "Their message is they're trying to get to everybody [to have], like, pretty much, peace, love and harmony. They want everything to work, their song is about that message. So, with 'Miracles,' they quit hiding the message, okay. All their older stuff they hid the message and a lot of people didn't get it. 'Miracles'... it's out there. It's like a slap in the face, you get the message. It's about the world. Everything's beautiful. They're not really saying screw science or anything. Scientists just are oblivious and, well, not all scientists, but some of them are pretty cool about it but a lot of scientists are oblivious and naive to the fact that miracles exist. They want fact for everything and there isn't fact for everything."

Fuckstick proceeds to tell me that even when ICP sang songs about more insidious things, the point was to push the message of peace and love: "Even the shit talking about killing, they're not really talking about going out and killing someone. They're rapping from someone else's perspective."

The duality of Wicked Shit (violent and mean-spirited lyrics promoting faith and love) confuses the outsider. When I tried to put myself in the mind of the Juggalo to figure it out, it only resulted in cognitive dissonance. Talking to them doesn't make it any clearer, but it illuminates why The Family doesn't have the same struggle with it. That any messages of love and faith are obtuse and untenable make it easy for Juggalos to piece the messages into something they are able to grasp. Add the Clown Love Juggalos receive from the Family and it's hard for them to dismiss any sacred or spiritual messages in the Dark Carnival. Somehow they make it work, but it's hard for the outsider to understand, perhaps because they go through the backdoor on a lot of things. Through objectification the Juggalos learn to appreciate different body types, through materialism they find sacrament, through violence they discover love, and through don't-give-a-fuck-nihilism they find faith. I think those notions explain why so many Juggalos told me if I really wanted to know about the Dark Carnival or Shangri-La I needed to ask every Juggalo, because it differs for everyone. Juggalos, however, don't ask anyone; the answers are in the Joker's Cards.

# KENTUCKY

Damon and I catch a few acts on the main stage, but mostly we just drink and run around. We manage to see Blaze Ya Dead Homie with about 15,000 Juggalos. Blaze's whole shtick is he's an ex-gangsta rapper who was killed and rose from the dead as a Juggalo to rap Wicked Shit. I smile and think of how that's an interesting metaphor for a lot of fallen off, old school rappers who jumped on the Juggalo bandwagon into an immediate captive fan base. Vanilla Ice received a great amount of respect from the 'los. Ice-T hosted a documentary about the Gathering called *ICP: A Family Underground*, and ICP features him on a few songs. Most notoriously, Coolio went as far as getting a tattoo that spelled "Juggalo" wrong.

For the record, Blaze, like a lot of acts we've seen out here, puts on a good show. While I'm not entirely sure I'd see him in a different context, he deserves props. Next up Twiztid, tonight's headliner, performs. I'm curious to see them, as they're second only to ICP in the Psychopathic Records Family.

Jamie Madrox, a fat white guy, and Monoxide Child, a skinnier white guy, comprise Twiztid. Together they rap about sex, violence, and alienation in a juvenile way with a lot of Gothic imagery. To distinguish themselves from ICP, they paint their faces completely white and wear eye contacts, which give them beady black and menacing pupils. They keep their hair short with little braids on top, a style they made popular among the Juggalos.

We watch them play a few songs, less than half a set, then they bless the audience by allowing them to hear their latest album before anyone else... and walk off the stage. A whole lot of Juggalos wander off into the night, but the amount of Juggalos who stay and face a dark stage listening to the CD over the PA shocks me. A few fluorescent wands and glow sticks light up the night along with the soft light of the Midway, but it's really, really dark as the Juggalos stay to listen to a CD of their heroes... the ones they came thousands of miles to see. It's one of the strangest things I've ever witnessed.

As it gets darker, I lose Damon. He goes back to the van to crash out because his gout got to him. I head to the Drug Bridge because, from my understanding, it's a good place to mingle. I'm done taping for the night and quite a bit drunker. I sit on the rail of the bridge, happy to just observe the action in my buzzy state. A young 'lo named Kentucky breaks my spell and everything changes.

"Hey, ninja! Are you actually from Kentucky or are you just wearing the t-shirt?" he asks me about my deliberately non-descript t-shirt.

"Huh? What? Oh, yeah, I'm from Kentucky," I say, not ready to break down where I live now, or everywhere else I've lived in my life. Besides, I've spent plenty of time in Kentucky.

"Cool, I just wanted to ask you because they call me Kentucky, but I'm not from Kentucky. That's just what people call me."

He thrusts out his hand and shakes mine. We start talking. He hails from somewhere in Illinois, a town I've not heard of. He rocks a thick goatee about six inches long and an oversized Twiztid t-shirt hangs loosely over his thin frame. He's ecstatic to be out here with his Family. And he's more than ready to meet more Family (ironically, because that's how he met me).

"Yeah, I'm not really a Juggalo. I just came out here with my buddy because we like rap and we thought we'd check it out," I tell him.

"Fuck yeah, that's awesome," he replies. "It's fucking cool that you came out here and checked it out, man. What do you think of it so far?"

"I think it's pretty awesome. I really like what you have going on."

At this point I feel like I say this truthfully. I don't like everything I see, but I'm starting to appreciate the Family.

"Awesome," he says. "So who do you like? I mean, you know ICP, right?"

"Yeah," I say. "I know some of their stuff and like it. But, hell, I've been seeing Juggalos around my town and I thought I'd come out and see what you're all about. Hell, why not, right? I mean there's some good rap here."

"Man, that's cool. I'm glad you did. I like to put it this way: we're just like hippies except that we dress this way and we have our own thing going on. We're a family and we take care of each other. See that guy over there," he says, pointing out a young, long-haired, guy in a tie-dye shirt. "That's Sam. He's a hippie, but he came out with us. He's our buddy, but he goes to festivals and sells shit, you know? But he's cool here. Nobody fucks with you here, man. I mean, there's some real douchebag Juggalos out here but most of us just want to show Clown Love. I mean, out there we aren't free. Here we're free."

"Are you really free here? I mean, sure, you can buy and do drugs out here, but are you free?"

"Well, there's a loophole here that lets us get away with this," he says, referring to the fact cops aren't allowed to come on the property because it's private. "But no, we're not even really free here. But this is where we feel free to just be together with our Family and to be ourselves, away from the bullshit. And that's what it's about, Clown Love. Now I know a lot of the lyrics are really violent, but that's just how we get our aggression out. Sometimes things are so fucked up that I feel like I want to kill somebody. You know? This music's good for getting that out, but really we're just like hippies, we just want to show Clown Love and take care of each other like a family."

We talk for a long time. I tell him that I came up in punk rock and got involved in punk for some of the same reasons.

"My older brother was punk," he says. "He taught me all about it. I think that shit's cool."

"But you found your own thing."

"Yeah."

He laughs at my beer, a tall can of shwill called Beer Thirty with the slogan "It's Beer Thirty somewhere" imprinted on the can.

"Ninja, we've been seeing those cans laying all over the place around here and we thought it was hilarious. Beer thirty!"

"Yeah, this shit is all we have to drink. We found a bunch of it on closeout." I hold the can out in front of him. "Here, man, try it."

Kentucky takes a drink,

"Yeah, ninja, it's not that bad… I guess."

"Not when put up against other shit our broke asses have gotten drunk on."

"No shit, right?' he says and laughs loudly. "Dude, you're awesome! I'm so glad I came up and asked you about your shirt, man. I'm going to tell everyone about you, man. I'm so glad you're here," he says emphatically as he turns to leave.

"Don't do that. I'll get my ass kicked for being a Juffalo!" I shout back.

"Man, you ain't no Juffalo. You're just an old punk rocker."

He turns a few yards off and yells back, waving off my self-deprecation.

I remember Kentucky long after I leave, and I feel I will betray him when I start writing about all of this. He's just a good guy. He doesn't want me to get down with the Clown. He just wants me to respect his people and where they come from. His exuberance and willing exposition is just what I wanted to experience among the Juggalos. It's the first time I realize how much I will betray these folks who were kind to me and respected me. I will criticize their leaders, and it doesn't matter what I say in favor of the Family, because being critical of Violent J and Shaggy will probably be seen as a betrayal, whether or not it's my intention.

# FOUR CORNERSTONES OF JUGGALO ATTRACTION

*We'll never die alone,*

*Juggalos will carry on,*

*Swing our hatchets if we must,*

*Each and every one of us...*

> – Insane Clown Posse, "Juggalo Chant"

*There is an important difference between the words "loser"
and "outlaw." One is passive and one is active.*

> – Hunter S. Thompson

I 've said a lot about the aesthetics of Juggalo culture, how
appealing it is to the Juggalo while being completely
inaccessible and revolting to everyone else. What I started

to get clued into early on though, was that a future Juggalo has to already be susceptible to the long, bony, beckoning finger of the Wicked Clown. As much as some non-Juggalos might not want to admit it, this predisposition is not far off from feelings and desires we've had ourselves. Really, how far off is the defiant nature of punk rock, with its liberty spikes and safety pins, from painting yourself up like a clown? How many steps away is the Axl Rose-idolizing redneck chugging a Budweiser and shouting, "I don't give a fuuuck!" from a Juggalo shouting, "If I only could I'd set the world on fire, *Fuck the world!*" along with Violent J and Shaggy? At the core, most of what Juggalo culture offers is transgressive, which has an appeal to the poor, to the outcast, to the marginalized. It was something I picked up early on in my research and is totally being confirmed at The Gathering. I came up with The Four Cornerstones of Juggalo Attraction, starting with some initial draws and ending on what keeps one swinging their hatchet for life. The Four Cornerstones of Juggalo Attraction are the Wicked Clown Face, to be reviled, The Family, and The Dark Carnival.

## THE FIRST CORNERSTONE: THE WICKED CLOWN FACE

Let's say a young person, who falls outside the cruel standards of high school, becomes an outcast because they are too nerdy, too socially awkward, or maybe even too sociopathic. Physically, they may be too fat, too ugly, or too small. Maybe they are too poor and circumstantially wear raggedy clothes like Violent J. Maybe it's their home life. Maybe they're beaten or diddled senseless from a young age until their self-esteem shatters so much they don't stand a chance at fitting in with the popular, or even the other unpopular, kids at school. They are floobs and scrubs, and their life is a living hell. The floob sees an Evil Clown grinning from a t-shirt, and goes home and looks up the name of the band on the shirt. Or maybe the guy wearing the t-shirt takes them in, sends them home with some burnt CDs of Insane Clown Posse and Twiztid. The floob gets it. The music serves as a vessel for their anger, the extreme violence an outlet for all the times they are picked on and unable to defend themselves. The Clown attracts them because the Clown doesn't give a fuck. The Clown is marginalized because it's violent, psychopathic, and insane. This misfit starts to see themself in that Clown face. They join the Juggalo family, embody that evil clown face, and their marginalization becomes voluntary. They portray themselves as violent, wicked, and they'll split your wig if you fuck with them. Don't fuck with a Juggalo.

## THE SECOND CORNERSTONE: TO BE REVILED

Identifying as a Juggalo means shedding involuntary marginalization for a marginalization of choice. The Juggalo gets tight with their Family and revels in their outcast status. They feel they are involved in something so dark, violent, and edgy that the rest of the world simply never understands. They love the hatred they receive from those outside the Dark Carnival. They see through evil Clown eyes now. It doesn't matter that most haters of Wicked Shit judge it on unintelligent and violent lyrics, or crass merchandising, or perhaps aren't buying the spiritual message, think painting faces up is kind of goofy, or don't care to be covered in soda pop. Maybe haters call ICP's music misogynistic or wish to further deconstruct it. But the Juggalos know the world will never understand the obscured positive message behind it all. The Juggalo only becomes more headstrong through this hate, swinging the hatchet because they must.

## THE THIRD CORNERSTONE: THE FAMILY

The Family offers important security and gives Juggalos the community they seek. Welcomed into an elite group of outcasts, they obtain a family of people who really understand them, unlike the abusive one at home. They no longer walk the hallways in their high schools alone with their head down, getting their asses kicked. Now they twist their fingers up in the shape of the Wicked Clown symbol and shout *"Whoop! Whoop!"* with all their fellow 'los. They will never die alone. Juggalos will carry on. They're close to the Juggalos in their town, but they also know 'los all over the country have their back. The Family is warm, treats them well, and accepts them for who they are. The Family is strong and takes care of their own. The Juggalo feels Clown Love and never wants to leave.

## THE FOURTH CORNERSTONE: THE DARK CARNIVAL

The Dark Carnival seals the deal. The rest of the world doesn't comprehend the Juggalos' faith, just as they don't understand anything about the Juggalos—only the Family understands. The trickiness of how the Dark Carnival faith works confuses and eludes me as always, but why it works is starting to make sense. The genius of ICP—they believe in something absurd and kooky, but as masters of self-promotion they can easily package and market it with expert precision. When I first began to research, I flipped back and forth between thinking they really believed in their Dark Carnival, and that they were just having us on. In the end, it seems like a bit of both. Just like they manipulate the Juggalos, it seems they fool themselves as well.

One thing to take into account when considering the influence of the Dark Carnival is that Violent J has publicly acknowledged his mental-health issues. Besides the fact that he based his entire career on an incident of hallucinating clowns in his living room, he also says he experiences panic attacks where he hears demons speaking to him and telling him he's going to hell. He's talked about being highly medicated, depressed, and prone to nervous breakdowns. Considering his background of childhood abuse and trauma, it's not really surprising. Nonetheless, everything that makes the Juggalos think Violent J is onto something and getting visions from God would strike non-Juggalo laymen as the ramblings of a delusional man. His religious fervor reminds me a lot of the psychology of geniuses, such as Van Gogh and Dostoyevsky, who were both prone to anxiety, manias, religious revelations, and psychotic breakdowns. Any kook who sees weird shit that isn't there could attempt to start a religion, though usually they wander the streets mumbling to themselves or shouting their doctrine to nonplussed and disinterested passers-by. But Violent J has charisma—Wicked Clown charisma. This draws the Juggalos in.

For the non-Juggalo who looks in on the Dark Carnival or watches the "Miracles" video, there's a whole lot of evidence that ICP is just plain stupid. But maybe it's not a matter of *how* intelligent they are, but how *they are* intelligent. Sure, it's easy to dismiss them because of their anti-intellectualism and puerile lyrics, but they created a whole Wicked Clown empire.

The contradictory nature of Psychopathic Records and Wicked Shit is a slippery, confused (and confusing) reality, to say the least. But it simply works because it's always adaptable. Violent J feels called to teach God's message, but he doesn't necessarily believe in the Bible's definition of sin. Without the gospel, ICP takes the "righteousness" in scripture and strips it of all accountability. With no solid guidelines for behavior, the Dark Carnival adapts to the lifestyle of the follower. And while it may be easy to suspect ICP are just having us on, upon deeper inspection it doesn't seem to be the case. ICP created a religion, not unlike a long line of religious zealots, that justifies all their behavior (if they just tweak it here and there). For instance, for all the justified hatred of "richies" in their songs and culture, Violent J and Shaggy will never be held accountable for their own wealth, or for gaining it by exploiting their disenfranchised followers. Psychopathic Records, indeed.

So the Dark Carnival is the final hook. A lot of Juggalos I talk to don't trust mainstream religion. Some even feel harmed by it. But a more adaptable religion just may be something to help them get through life, especially if it comes with the Wicked packaging. Once they're "down with the Clown," tight with their homies, and proudly withdrawn from society, they become receptive to the Dark Carnival's message.

# ANTI-INTELLECTUALISM

*How many times did I walk in and just sit?*

*And have to listen, and learn all this bullshit*

*Learnin' history and science, fuckin' wait*

*Knowin' that, will that put food on my plate?*

— Insane Clown Posse, "How Many Times"

After this Gathering, ICP appears on a talk show called *Attack of the Show.* The show's host asks Violent J and Shaggy what they do at the end of the day after they take off the makeup. "Is [sic] there geopolitical discussions?"

"I don't even know what geopolitical means," Violent J, in grinning face paint, replies with unsettling delight.

He disturbingly announces this with what seems to be a certain degree of pride, as if it's cool or noble to be this naive.

This is why everyone yucks it up over the "Miracles" video. It's not the fact that the video is spiritual, despite what ICP claims. (Violent J has said that if Bob Dylan wrote a song like "Miracles" critics would rave about it. However, Dylan's fundamentalist period was his most unpopular era.) No, the reason everyone makes a joke of the song is because Shaggy 2 Dope thinks scientists lie to him, which pisses him off. In their music, they seem to harbor a vigorous desire to remain ignorant and to keep the Juggalos ignorant. While I have a begrudging respect for their areas of expertise—self-promotion and creating controversy constructive to building their empire—their message carries a very strong sense of anti-intellectualism.

"Stupid people can get more accomplished, because smart people will talk themselves out of it," opines Damon about ICP's success.

It's hard to argue with that when hearing songs of theirs like "Stuck Her with My Wang," where they sing about gluing a woman's titties to the roof with Elmer's Glue. Violent J and Shaggy really push the floob-pride agenda, but not necessarily as a means to a better end. In his autobiography, Violent J raves about how he didn't give a fuck about school or his studies, how he fucked off and wasted those years and it all paid off because he and Shaggy made millions as rapping clowns. But what does this leave for Juggalos? He just encourages 'los to follow the Dark Carnival. As much as ICP talks about how they love their followers, it's essential they remain just that: followers.

In a section of the book where J describes how they hated and abused groupies because groupies weren't after anything but a piece of their wealth and fame, he makes a disclaimer saying he isn't referring to all women, and certainly not Juggalettes. He says he "can most readily relate to the Juggalettes" (which may easily translate to "I only relate to women who talk about me"). There's a subtext to this misogyny; Violent J needs to be in a position where the balance of power is in his favor. You can see this throughout ICP's art and actions.

•　　　•　　　•

I'm a self-educated, self-published, DIY (do-it-yourself), ex-punk kid exposed to a much broader underground culture after being empowered by the intellectual side of punk rock. There are two main routes a punk kid can take. One of the many opportunities presented to me was drinking 40-ounces of malt liquor, slamming dope, sitting in the street bumming for change all day, and listening to The Exploited. But on the flipside of that coin, there's always been punk's intellectual side —which encourages self-ascension and resists the establishment, the state, and following leaders. There was always a part of punk that resisted nihilism and embraced its DIY ethics. Knowing that things were fucked and that punks couldn't count on society to offer them anything, they worked on making their own community, one that was more in line with what they wanted to see. They created zines, collectives, community centers, needle exchanges, and made their own venues. Punk exposed you to ideas and encouraged you to act on them. From there, one can go anywhere. It's this side of punk that encourages young people to better themselves. None of this could have come about though, in a subculture of top-down leadership.

The Family is similar to punk, because it's a community for folks who don't have one, and both were based around taking pride in one's ostracization. Punk is also fueled by negativity— owning it, and turning it into positive energy. The difference is ICP's vested interest in the 'los *staying* floobs. ICP is being manipulative by not encouraging the 'los to find their own path, because that path might lead them away from being a Juggalo.

When Violent J describes his "long goodbye to the Ferndale educational system" in his autobiography, he writes, "motherfuckin' fuck school. I'm 31 years old, today, screamin' fuck school. It wasn't for me after eighth grade." And it wasn't. School is an oppressive place for a lot of kids, especially the poor and working class. Poorly-paid teachers and administrators in inner-city schools often target youth who come from bad homes because they act out or just don't know how to act. These teachers may resent their jobs and their place in life and decide to take it out on the kids, trying to drag them down with them. Violent J describes a day when he basically just spaced out, got up during class, and starting chucking volumes of an encyclopedia out the window. His teacher pulled him to the front of the class and tore him down in front of everybody.

"This kid right here is gonna amount to nothing. You're never going to do anything, Mr. Bruce, are you? You'll come to school your whole life, and you'll never do anything here, will you? You know that? I'll bet that, don't you, Mr. Bruce? Everybody look at this kid. This is Joe. He is happy with himself even though he is gonna mean nothing at all to the world. He will be a nothing. He will never be anything in the world." Violent J recounts his teacher saying these things way back then.

"To me," Violent J continues, "I was the freshest kid there. I loved that fresh moment in the spotlight. I loved that fresh moment when he said my whole life will be as worthless as a grain of salt. I loved *always* being the underdog. It was my whole motto as a true floob, a scrub, a Juggal—Not yet."

The Juggalos I talk to love these stories, but few hold success stories of their own. They have trouble making even common conversation without bringing Violent J or Shaggy into it. They live vicariously through ICP's underdog story and through consumerism, crudely attempting to insert themselves into that success story. But the rapping clown is a tapped market, and though a whole lot of Juggalos may put on the makeup and rap evil threats to haters, I doubt they're going to make out like ICP. But I don't think ICP cares about this. Perhaps Insane Clown Posse was an idea that's time had come; perhaps they're true underdogs who saved themselves from poverty. And there is pride in making your own trail after being rejected, making yourself a success by your own rules. And sure, Violent J shouldn't have stuck around in school if it was that hellish for him.

But even if Violent J managed to find a way around an education, an elevation of the mind is almost always necessary to rise above. Just because he's come this far by rapping about "getting butt-naked and walking through the streets winking at the freaks with a 2-liter stuck in his butt cheeks," doesn't mean the Juggalos can reach this level of success (ironically, he relays this sentiment in the song "What is a Juggalo?"). I'm not saying Violent J should study geopolitics if big words offend him (hell, I know what geopolitics means, but I still have trouble making rent), nor should Shaggy 2 Dope look up magnets on Wikipedia if he doesn't care to know how they work. It's worked for them so far. However, their followers may not have the privilege to slide by in life on greasepaint and religious epiphany. To encourage stupidity on the people who look up to them seems irresponsible and exploitative, and doing so while selling them Hatchet Gear and multiple editions of the same album with limited edition tracks makes it seem even more insidious, especially when I see the Juggalos hawk them for gas in order to get home from the Gathering. But making such accusations denies Violent J of his prophecy and ICP of their Dark Carnival calling. Nonetheless, they only encourage Juggalos to be Juggalos, not Juggalo lawyers or doctors, not Juggalo grassroots organizers, Juggalo feminists, or even literate Juggalos. For a Juggalo to better him or herself, it almost seems they must leave it all behind: the Juggalo Family, the Wickedness, the Dark Carnival, and even Shangri-La. That's quite a bit to ask.

I've heard more than one Juggalo claim to have met a brain surgeon at The Gathering. I'm dying to meet this brain surgeon, because that would be one case where a Juggalo broke from the adherence to the floobs-for-life doctrine. I'm sure some Juggalos have, but the standard is disheartening. Still, I think there's beauty in the way the Juggalos take pride in being outcasts and being poor, the way they own it. It reminds me of how the filthy and shocking aesthetics of punk rock allowed me—a weird, poor kid—to gain some self-respect and self-esteem, and to take pride in my alienation. I'm just glad it didn't end there.

But what if a Juggalo were to take an interest in geopolitics, despite Violent J's lack thereof? Would they still take as much interest in Wicked Shit? Would the family accept this growth? Would anyone listen to them with all that clown paint on?

. . .

I'm watching the Neden Game in the Bomb Tent. "Neden" in Juggalo slang means pussy, and I'm basically watching a version of that old TV show *The Bachelor Game*. A tarp separates three male contestants on one side of the stage from an empty chair waiting to be filled by a female contestant. Ron Jeremy, decked out in a Hawaiian shirt, hosts the event.

"We need a Juggalette," he says, and a bunch of hands go up amidst shouts of *"Whoop! Whoop!"*

Jeremy's assistant, a mustached, middle-aged, stagehand goes into the audience and comes back with a large—no, a very large—contestant. She wears her tank top pulled up and around the back of her neck, exposing a huge belly and long, pendulous breasts. He sits her down in the metal folding chair on the other side of the tarp, hidden from the Juggalos to start the game.

Jeremy shakes his head.

"You're an asshole," he says.

He looks down, still shaking his head, then with a bewildered look asks the contestant a little bit about herself.

She tells us where she's from and what she does, and then announces she's married. "My husband's out there," she says pointing to the audience. "He's okay with this."

"You're an asshole," Ron Jeremy repeats to his assistant, who looks sheepish but says nothing.

"I need a question from the audience," Ron Jeremy says and points to someone.

"Ask them what their job is."

"I'm in construction," Contestant One says.

"I'm self-employed," Contestant Two answers with a wink. The crowd taunts him playfully.

"Yeah, right," Ron Jeremy says skeptically.

"I work in a kitchen," Contestant Three says.

The questions are kind of basic, and when asked how they make love, one of them pulls out some nasty, wicked, sexy talk. Contestant Two says he likes to take it slow and easy when pleasing a woman.

"I'm going to have to go with what Contestant Two said," says Contestant Three creatively.

I can't stop staring at the back of a bright, blue-haired head in front of me. It belongs to a child who couldn't be more than eleven, arms crossed and leaning against the stage watching the game. Somebody suggests a dance-off rated by the *Whoop! Whoop!*-ing of the crowd; Contestant Three wins.

"Another question from the audience," Ron Jeremy says.

The blue-haired child raises his hand. Ron Jeremy notices him and holds the mic out so he can propose a question to the topless woman.

"Ask them if they like fat chicks," he says.

"I can do with a little cushion in my pushin'," Contestant One says.

"I can appreciate some big-girl love," Contestant Two says.

"Me too, it's all good," Contestant Three says.

When all the questions are done and it comes down to the decision, the Juggalette chooses Contestant Number Three. The two come from around the tarp and meet. Any shock at her size has been dulled by the kid's question, or possibly didn't matter anyway. The winner walks off the stage with his married date, escorting her to a helicopter ride.

*"Whoop! Whoop!"* goes the crowd.

"You're an asshole," Ron Jeremy says to his assistant one more time.

# THE WICKED CLOWN FACE AND THE REBEL FLAG

*Teachin' kids what pops taught you,*

*And he's a funky-ass bigot, too,*

*Fell short of the due respect,*

*Don't speak when I slap ya in your redneck,*

*Fuck all that bullshit you stuck on,*

*Get back on your mule and get the fuck on,*

*Don't look back or I'm a hit ya,*

*Take that redneck bitch out with ya,*

*Spit on your Rebel rag, so fuck you and your Rebel flag!*

—Insane Clown Posse, "Your Rebel Flag"

*We be the all doing, the all-seeing, the all knowing*

*Chainsaw, baseball bat, and axe toting*

*Eastside, white trash with tattoos*

*This is how the fuck we live*

*This is what the fuck we do.*

—Twiztid, "White Trash Wit Tat-2's"

*I don't give a fuuuuck!*

—White trash saying

Insane Clown Posse's song "Your Rebel Flag" is a murderous call-out to racist rednecks, particularly those in the South. The chorus simply repeats "Fuck your rebel flag" over and over. The song isn't very nuanced. Clearly you don't have to be from the South or rural areas to be racist, but the Juggalos seem to know is being targeted by the song: racists and bigots, skinheads, and the KKK. It helps that ICP has enough sense to clarify, "Straight folks in the South won't have it/They put a round in your racist ass quick/The cool in the south team up with the north/And blow that bigot off his fucking horse."

Racist rednecks may be a worthy target for violence, but that isn't what I find interesting about the song. Nor is it the hypocrisy of their militantly anti-bigoted stance when they seem completely oblivious of their own bigotry toward women and queer folks. I take these things into consideration, but what's really compelling to me is their fixation on the symbol of their targets: the Confederate flag. Perhaps you have to come from a place where people fly that flag to pick up on it, but there are many parallels between the Rebel Flag and the evil clown face— all having to do with the personal meaning individuals project onto these symbols.

In the song, ICP defines a "redneck" as a racist white guy who lives in the rural South: "What you say ain't always hype/So I slap you in the face with a lead pipe/Teachin' kids what pops taught you/And he's a funky ass bigot too/Fell short of the due respect/Don't speak when I slap ya in your redneck/ Fuck all that bullshit you stuck on/Get back on your mule and get the fuck on." By taking this stance, they draw clear lines. As accepting as The Family is, they aren't down with racists. A young white kid might really like ICP and all this Wicked Shit he's hearing, he might think the Hatchet Gear is fly, but he must make a choice between what pops taught him—racist ideas that might be all he knows—and being a Juggalo.

But the term "redneck" itself belongs less to a specific region, and applies more to poor, white, uneducated people anywhere in the States. If ICP were to do a tour of small towns north of the Mason-Dixon Line, they may find quite a few poor, white folks who also identify with the Confederate flag, just like they may find a lot of Juggalos in the South who identify with the Wicked Clown face. Still, it is ironic in light of all ICP's railing against hicks and rednecks that the rural poor are the people who make up such a huge portion of their fanbase.

In my experience in small towns I've lived in, rednecks (or white trash) are often drawn to a machismo front, to transgressive imagery that is rebellious, tough, and "badass." They latch onto Marlboro cigarettes, keeping packs of them rolled up in the sleeves of Marlboro logo t-shirts, which they acquire with coupons peeled from the side of the packs. Their Looney Tune of choice is Taz, who is emblazoned on hats and boxer shorts. I saw them love this rowdy, unstoppable force of nature over the more conniving Bugs Bunny—or even the blustering, gun-toting Yosemite Sam—because Taz is so far beyond taming, a complete wild id that they see in themselves. Their favorite band was almost always Guns N' Roses, and Axl, an Indiana boy himself, was the baddest motherfucker ever. They loved his volatility, wore their hair long like him, and imitated his cocksure bluster and explosive rage. Perhaps the last example dates me. When I was doing my time in Southern Indiana there was no Insane Clown Posse or Wicked Clowns.

Among all these symbols, and not just in the South, the Rebel Flag is also worn, hung in windows, and flown from trucks. In my head right now, I can hear a redneck somewhere wearing a Confederate bandana proclaiming loudly in an accent I've often imitated, "I don' give a fuuuck!" The profanity drawled out for a nihilist effect. This dude is an archetype I've run into plenty of times. The odds are good that this guy is racist. He's obviously not anti-racist, or he would have enough compassion to not wear a symbol that's threatening to Black people. But my argument is not for the morality of this archetype. I just want to make the case, from my experience, that their attachment to the Confederate flag is primarily because it makes them feel badass. I'm basing my arguments north of the Mason-Dixon, because it's not only where I've had a lot of my experience with Rebel Flag wavers, but it also takes it out of the context of Southern pride, "heritage not hate," and any of the other mythologies around the Confederate flag. I agree with ICP that most folks who wave this flag around have little respect for Black people. Plenty of them are probably nonverbally racist, but it's just not true that all of them fly it as a symbol of white supremacy. Every person I've had the misfortune of crossing paths with, wears it because it makes them feel like…a rebel. To them the Rebel Flag is transgressive, and it marks them as being so. By wearing it they're challenging everyone they meet.

Besides a hyper-masculine ignorance, it also betrays a distinct lack of culture. Poor, white people are often landless, living in trailer parks and shacks. Their inheritance: crystal meth and welfare. It's already applied to them. They glob onto this symbol and ascribe meaning to it because of a cultural void. People already assume they're uneducated and ignorant, so there's a degree of ownership to flying the flag—even if it doesn't represent their part of the country or their ancestor's side in the war.

The Wicked Clown face works in a similar way to the Confederate flag (you could even call it a healthy alternative). As much as the Confederate flag is a confused symbol—getting even murkier as it crosses the Mason-Dixon—everyone damn well knows it's been a symbol for slavery for a lot of people. It's a symbol of oppression and disunity; the flag-waver must be somewhat okay with that, no matter what meaning they apply to it. For poor white kids who are drawn to the Wicked Clown, it comes from the same place, it appeals to the same sense of disenfranchisement. While I've made the effort to dispel the stereotype that the Juggalo Family is a strictly white subculture, there's no fucking way the Juggalo Family would be as big as it is today if ICP and Wicked Shit didn't resonate with poor, white people—their core audience.

No matter what subculture someone chooses to get into (punk, metal, hippie, etc.) they're always better off than a Juggalo. Nobody but a Juggalo can understand wearing clown paint on a regular basis, or the depth of the song "Bugz on My Nugz." The Juggalo aesthetic repulses everyone who isn't a Juggalo. Even punks who appreciate someone like GG Allin, who would take Ex-Lax and then throw shit on his audience, are put-off by Juggalo culture. Somebody already outcast by society who becomes a Juggalo does so because everyone else hates it. Feeding on this negative attention, they ultimately win. Getting a rise out of how the garish and dark aesthetic of the clown alienates them from the rest of society, these same folks who may be called hicks, trailer trash, and rednecks now identify as proud Juggalos. To be a Juggalo is to be a target of ridicule from everyone, but it allows them the ownership of that ridicule. They grow stronger from any attacks they incur because they have the Family to turn to.

The Wicked Clown face for the Juggalo comes from the exact same drive that makes the redneck claim the Rebel Flag as their symbol. Both are symbols of power for groups of people who are dehumanized, stripped of culture, and denied upward mobility. There comes a point when someone is done arguing that they aren't white trash or poor or stupid because of where they come from, or the way they talk or the way they let it all hang out, and they start wearing the things they are ridiculed for like a badge of honor.

# WICKED LAISSEZ-FAIRE

*Charlie Brown, please, don't come around*

*Because your weed is doodoo brown*

*and it smells like the ground*

                    –ABK (Anybody Killa), "Charlie Brown"

"*Fuck the beach! Fuck the beach!*" the ninjas on the dock chant to those on the beach.

"*Fuck the dock! Fuck the dock!*" the ninjas on the beach chant to those on the dock.

The chants continue as the two sides do battle. Barrages of plastic bottles fly back and forth. This battle never ends, renewed by a revolving door of Juggalos who take up sides based on whichever one is nearest to them. Damon and I have spent a long time on the beach, getting in and out of Lake Hepatitis to cool off, and the fight never ceases. Some of the Juggalos chant and throw shit for up to three hours.

"You got a stupid hat!" a skinny 'lo floating near the beach yells, throwing a bottle at a fat, shirtless, hairy guy on the dock wearing an enormous straw hat.

I start laughing out loud at this and Damon turns to me, smiles his canine smile, and repeats it.

"You got a stupid hat," he says, and this is another moment I'm glad to share with my best friend.

Our levity catches the attention of a Latino ninja from Florida, who walks over to us. "Can I film you guys and ask you a question?" he asks.

"Sure," Damon says, and I nod to him.

"What do you guys think of The Gathering so far?" he asks, looking through the lens of a small digital camera.

Damon and I tell him we're having a great time.

"Did you get any hoes?" he asks. I look away. Damon, closer to him, does the talking.

"Well, it seems all the cute ones got boyfriends and the rest... aren't so hot... "

Richie puts his phone camera to his side and says, "Yeah, Juggalettes aren't known for being very hot." He pauses. "I'm Richie," he says and shakes our hands.

Richie just arrived today from Florida and has spent his time wandering around asking this question, saying he's going to post the results as a film on YouTube when he gets home. We tell him it's awesome to be out here. After chatting for a few more minutes, he tells us to hold on, runs a few yards off, and comes back with a collapsible camp chair like Damon's. He sets it down next to Damon's chair as I sit further back on a towel. It's his second Gathering.

"How was Twiztid?" he asks.

"They were good," Damon says, "but they only played for 15 minutes."

"Yeah, that's what I heard," Richie says, then asks how the new CD sounded.

"We didn't listen to it," Damon replies.

Richie asks what we thought of Psychopathic Rydas and other bands who played. Eventually, the conversation comes around to how everyone hocks something out here.

"At concerts and festivals we've gone to, there's always a bunch of parasites that sit around and beg for change, booze, drugs, or whatever. Here nobody's even asked me for a cigarette. It's really a shock," I say.

"Everybody here is a hustler," Richie says. "Everybody out here has some kind of caper going on."

We tell Richie that's one of the first things we noticed—how everything constantly turns over here. Lightly-used ICP jerseys sell for drugs, which sell for booze, which sells for glow-in-the-dark hatchets, which sell for titty flashes. The ingenuity of the Juggalos' resourcefulness amazes us. While most of the cash floats up to the top—obvious from the amount of Hatchet Gear we see at The Gathering—quite a bit still floats around from Juggalo to Juggalo on a lower rung of commerce. The printed program about The Gathering listed a lot of restricted items:

glass bottles and the like. Since it's our first Gathering, we did our best not to bring anything on the restricted list, for fear we wouldn't get in. Most concerts and festivals of this size overflow with rules and regulations, to which organizers stringently adhere to avoid lawsuits. But at the Gathering it's clear nobody really gives a damn. Everybody knows they can do whatever the hell they want, so Juggalos save and scam up enough money to get down here, and then ball whatever they can to cover costs once they arrive.

It's as much a part of the culture as ignoring everything else in the program—from no throwing things to no fireworks to no glass bottles. Just about every "rule" proves irrelevant. People set up booths hustling everything you might forget, from sunscreen to ice cold beer to blunt wraps. This part of Juggalo culture may trickle down from its hip hop roots, but maybe it stems more from the fact that Juggalos are usually underclass. It's not something I'm used to; I'm used to the parasitic element of counterculture: crusty punks and hippies who come out to leech everything they can. They travel from festival to festival all year round to sit in one spot with busy foot traffic and beg for other people's stuff, and I have come to expect it. Too lazy to join society, they come up with some kind of wishy-washy, pseudo-political justification to plague the fringes.

"I couldn't buy a ticket, so me and my ninjas snuck in here. A lot of ninjas do," a Juggalette says. "Since I've been out here ninjas have been taking care of me with food n' shit."

Her story says something about the Juggalo Family. The 'los who ask for a bit of help get what they need—from each according to their abilities to each according to their needs.

There's a dignity Juggalos have in this sense which I have yet to see anywhere else.

However, there is a limit to the hustling, and that's when it cuts into the profits of ICP. As Damon and I walk back to the van from Lake Hepatitis, we see some Juggalos call out a dumpy, creep-mustached, middle-aged man about 20-years older than them.

"You guys want to buy some stickers?" the older man asks with a handful of decals. "Fuck you, get the hell out of our Gathering," one of the Juggalos shouts at him.

"I'll go wherever I want," he responds.

"Nobody wants your shit, fuck off!" yells the other 'lo.

I like plenty of bands, really like them, but I don't give a damn if they lose money on some stickers. But Juggalos protect ICP's profits, even if it's a fraction of a cent from some lousy stickers.

# THE INSANE CLOWN POSSE SEMINAR

*Seminar (n.) a small group, or course, for advanced study.*

*–The New American Webster Handy College Dictionary*

In the blazing sun, countless Juggalos are amassed around the Seminar Tent. The crowd is so dense that outside the tent I can't see those inside taking up the hay-bale seating, let alone the stage. Inside, Violent J and Shaggy 2 Dope hold their seminar.

I listen for a while as they talk about their upcoming tour and CDs coming out on Psychopathic Records. They talk about the wrestling auditorium they are building in Detroit. They just promote and promote for most of an hour. Then Violent J gives away fly shoes to 'los who correctly answer trivia questions about ICP. According to him, the shoes are worth $800 and he's worn the pair only a few times.

"If you wash them up they'll be fresh," he says.

I think about how much an $800 pair of shoes might fetch me on eBay. Could I get more if Violent J once wore them?

The next thing they talk about is throwing shit.

"Who thinks this year's no-throwing-shit policy is lame? Who thinks that?" Violent J asks.

A big cheer comes up from the crowd, mixed with some booing.

"Who's for this year's no throwing shit rule?"

A bigger cheer goes up.

"I know everybody's talking about throwing shit at Tila Tequila…" Violent J goes on.

Some *"Whoop! Whoop!"*'s come up from a good portion of the crowd.

"I want y'all to think about this," Violent J continues.

"Hey, I'm trying to fuck that bitch. She's lame, but she's hot," Shaggy butts in, his clown grin taking on a weird predatory context.

"We brought her here with the intentions of seeing something you don't see every day," Violent J explains. "And that's Tila Tequila up there rapping. You're gonna do what you want to do and we're gonna love you regardless, but we just want you to know…"

"And I'm trying to fuck that bitch!" Shaggy repeats.

"And if you throw shit at her, there's no chance Shaggy's gonna fuck her. You can guarantee that," says Violent J.

"You get the logic," Shaggy says, pantomiming with a swing of his arm. "I'll throw my dick at her."

"And we want Shaggy to be able to fuck that bitch," Violent J says, reiterating their instructions.

The Juggalos agree with some "*Whoop! Whoop!*"s.

"And if you throw shit at the wrestling," Violent J continues, "you're going to make the matches shitty, man."

Shaggy and Violent J explain why it's not cool to throw stuff at the wrestlers; it makes the ring wet and the wrestlers screw up their moves.

With that final point the seminar ends and a huge "*Whoop! Whoop!*" rises from the Juggalos.

"That's it?" I wonder to myself.

With the seminar over, I move on to watch Juggalo Class Wrestling, ICP's wrestling league. ICP spares no skrilla on the Hard Knox Wrestling stage. It's elevated and surrounded by bleachers, and even has a long red runway for a grand entrance. I sweat in the heat and swig on a jug of water as I watch the match. A heel in a police uniform who calls himself Officer Colt Cabana taunts the crowd, "I pulled a bunch of you faggots over on the way in and I made my quota and then some."

The crowd boos him in mock distaste. He points the butt of a Mag Light into the crowd. "I will now start the first annual Gathering of the Juggalos D.A.R.E concept. Keep children and Juggalos off of drugs. I dare you to get a job. I dare you to get out of your mother's basements. I dare you to go to a dentist, young kid. I dare you to stop sucking everyone's dick young lady. I dare you to get a haircut…"

The crowd screams epithets back at the wrestler.

"And I dare you to stop being a Mexican!" Colt shouts and points.

"*Oooohhhh!*" the Juggalos retort in unison.

Racism gets 'em. Colt turns it onto the referee.

"And you call yourself an official. This is a Black man in charge. I can only assume you are the sole reason for the drugs spread all around this campground."

Now the Juggalos just go crazy booing and ranting, shouting back at Officer Colt. Bottles fly at the stage, but other 'los regulate these shit-throwing ninjas quickly. They're singled out and regulated with a quick chant of "*Don't throw shit!*" barely interrupting the wrestler's script.

"I believe each and every one of you Juggalos are human pieces of shit and when I'm done with arresting you I will arrest Violent J and Shaggy 2 Dope. I will put them in jail and I will fuck them in their ass, because that's what a good cop does."

He presses a thick, pink, rubber dildo to the crotch of his khakis, walks to the turnbuckle, stands on the ropes, thrusts his hips, and gets some laughs from the crowd. Am I the only one here wondering where the hell the dildo came from? Because I didn't notice it before. Did a Juggalo throw it on the stage? Or did he have it stashed somewhere? Not that it matters, even with all the rule-breaking Juggalos throwing things; the whole thing is an act, an exchange between the audience and the wrestler. It's appropriate that a "heel" wrestler at the Gathering of the Juggalos portrays a cop and a racist. It makes a point of the freedom the Juggalos feel here by setting up a parody of any authority besides ICP, and the fact that the Juggalos get really worked up when the wrestler's character reveals his racism and says something about the Family. The Family doesn't truck with racists. ICP won't have it. The Juggalos take their songs about fucking up racists and bigots seriously.

The term "post-racial" comes to mind. It's used to get away with putting disguised racism right out there in the open, and a cheap way to deny the fact people of color still face oppression. I'm hesitant to use the term "hipster" because the term means something different to everyone, but I can't help but think of the track-bike-riding, PBR-swilling faction of wealthy hipsters who recently discovered Juggalos as something else to make fun of. Hipsters famously make ironic, racist jokes to come off as edgy, and then call anyone who disagrees a "pussy" because they "can't take it." Meanwhile, they gentrify neighborhoods and live on trust funds while everybody else struggles to put food on the table. Only an idiot would say racism is over, just like it would take an idiot to be unaware of the poverty so many of us live in. But wealth hinders empathy.

If I've ever seen anything post-racial, it's this Dark Carnival. Everyone here is considered Family. Everybody here is a floob and equal. Everyone has similar ethics as dictated by ICP. Colt Cabana isn't being ironic; he's playing a role by being the "heel." We're supposed to hate him, and when the good guy comes out we root for him. Of course Colt knows what gets the Juggalos riled up, and he works it. Outside of The Gathering, a cop throwing down race bombs would offend Juggalos, but there are no cops here. He's just a bad-guy wrestler and all the 'los and 'lettes mock him in defense of racial harmony. Nothing is misunderstood. No sensitivities or sensibilities are fucked with. *Whoop! Whoop!*

This exemplifies one of the more positive ways Insane Clown Posse use their influence. Since they reach so many dispossessed white folks, they've likely swayed a lot of uneducated people to overcome their prejudiced backgrounds. Everything ICP says stands as the indisputable truth, from soda pop to politics. Violent J and Shaggy have done well by this; ICP claim they open a lot of minds through their strong anti-racist stance, and I've met quite a few Juggalos who back up these claims personally.

ICP reaches people where they are. Since most of their followers are disenfranchised, they feel it when ICP raps about killing child molesters and wife beaters and rich people. Hearing ICP rap about these issues may be the first time they've heard such issues addressed in a way that allows them to release their rage about stuff they and their loved ones deal with.

For a moment, I slip back into the past. I think about driving my best friend Tammy around when we were teenagers. I think about pulling my shitty Chevy LeBaron over on the side of a dusty rural route and holding her after we pulled away from her uncle's trailer.

"The guy who raped me was in there," she ran out bawling.

I knew the story already. She had already told me about how her older uncle, whom she looked up to, had given his 20-something drunk friend permission to rape her.

"Go do it," he said, too drunk to move from the couch. It was something I was reminded of every time she hit seek on the radio when that mic-stand-humping, jerk-off Steven Tyler of Aerosmith came on caterwauling about Janie having a gun and needing to "run, run away from the pai-ai-ain."

Plenty of 'heroes for the people' exist in the history of popular music, and plenty of rock stars speak for the poor and the wretched of the earth. But none of these musical heroes hit them quite like Violent J and Shaggy. It all adds up to one thing: ICP never quit speaking to the poor in their language. They gave them pride in themselves, in being scrubs and floobs. Then they gave them a Family and a Wicked Clown mask to shield them. Almost everything the Juggalos deal with, ICP has lived through. Violent J and Shaggy have that authenticity, the same authenticity which kept me from ever asking Tammy why she loved her uncle so much. Or why she would ever want to go back into that awful trailer again. Then I realize how easily I'm thinking about all this shit while watching a guy in a cop uniform wrestle a guy in a green and yellow jumpsuit after tossing a dildo into the crowd. Suddenly, I realize I just broke the code. And it all makes sense.

Though amused by the vulgar pre-match blustering, I am quickly bored of the match once it starts. I watched wrestling as a kid and I looked forward to checking it out here. What other event would I end up at that includes professional wrestling in the ticket price? But without all the different camera angles of television, it just seems slow and tedious. The wrestlers take forever to set up their moves, and the execution of them hardly impresses. Don't get me wrong, it's well done, top-of-the-line, pro wrestling, but I've outgrown the whole shtick and the weather makes it just too damn hot for entertainment. No matter how much water I drink, I feel miserable and nauseated. Finally it all gets to me, and I run around to the back of the bleachers and puke my guts out, distracting a few Juggalos from the match, and they shout, *"Whoop! Whoop!"*

Still dizzy from the heat, I head back to the van. I notice the Juggalos packing into the merch booth. A line of them snake out into the hot sun outside the autograph tent. Early this morning they started lining up around it, clutching posters, CDs, t-shirts, and whatever else to get signed by Psychopathic Records artists and other guests of The Gathering. The brown straw grass on the grounds, ugly before, is now completely obscured by garbage. Faygo bottles, empty nitrous balloons, discarded glow sticks, half-eaten elephant ears, greasy, marrowy bones of Jumbo Bitch Beaters, paper plates, tons of swag from Wicked Shit rappers, broken things, and glow-in-the-dark novelties that no longer glow in the dark litter the ground. The Juggalos seem oblivious to this eyesore of trash as they stand in line in the sun, but I can't help noticing it's everywhere. Sure, we're out on some crappy biker land, brown and brittle and dried out, and no one's really here to camp, but still—the amount of litter grosses me the fuck out.

I find Damon sitting in his collapsible lawn chair in the shade with his bad foot propped up inside the open van door, drinking beer and drawing Juggalos.

"Hey, one of you ninjas got a lighter?" a Juggalette asks, coming up to our van. "Hey, that's cool," she says looking over Damon's shoulder at his drawing. "You're awesome."

I dig a lighter out of the van, hand it to her, and she sparks up a bowl. She hands it to me, but I decline, telling her I have a piss test coming up.

"Aw, that sucks, ninja," she says and passes it to Damon, who hits it and hands it back.

She's from a town in Wisconsin I've never heard of, and it quickly slips my mind.

"I'll talk to you 'los," she says and walks off to her nearby camp with a "*Whoop! Whoop!*"

"*Whoop! Whoop!*" we shout back.

We crack open a couple of beers, wash down the Percocet Damon scored earlier from a teenager, and chill out by the van until the drugs kick in and the heat gets more tolerable. Juggalos come by—most just shouting "*Whoop! Whoop!*" but a few stop to say hello. Nathan and Samantha make an appearance and tell us about the Miss Juggalette contest.

"There was a Juggalette who was having dudes wrap dollar bills around their dicks and then she came around and took the dollars off with her mouth," Samantha says. "But then, she got beat out by a squirter who was squirting in guys' faces."

Jared and Mark drop in and out. Jared tells us of when he rapped with Shock G from Digital Underground a long time ago.

"They asked the crowd if anybody could rap. Well, I used to at the time, so my buddy pointed me out and I got pulled up on the stage by Shock G. I just picked out two girls at the front of the stage that seemed to be digging it and starting rapping to them, pretending they were the whole audience. I was pretty nervous." He smiles, taking another pull of his blunt and blowing the sweet fruity scent through the air.

As he talks, we try to figure out how to get Mark back into The Gathering. Last night he ripped his wristband off while tripping on acid. Crystal, a frail blonde with a nasty scar that curves up from her mouth for nearly three inches, is trying to help find a solution. She bribed gate security to let her in without a wristband by offering him several cans of beer. Then she cut off her own wristband and gave it to Mark so he could get in. Now we're trying to find a way to attach her wristband to Mark's wrist. We use my pocket knife to cut up a promo sticker of some clown rapper and tape the wristband together. Crystal doesn't really seem motivated for any reason other than to help Mark out. They don't even appear to know each other; she's just camped nearby. They go to the gate to try it out. It works, so they come back and we all hang out. We talk. We laugh. We tell stories. The sun will soon set and I'm feeling pretty drunk.

Overall, I like the Juggalos. Most of them are nice folks. A lot of them I would even call gentle, as people who've been kicked around a lot and don't fit in with the world often are. Take Jared, he's not much different from the guy who lives in your apartment building or down the block, the guy who occasionally swings by with a six pack. He talks about a lot more than Wicked Shit, making it easy to find common ground with him. I could easily see Damon and me befriending someone like Jared outside of The Gathering. But Juggalos like Jared are the minority. The difference is the level of dedication, and this where it gets tricky. Most Juggalos entrench themselves in the lifestyle. So for every Juggalo like Jared whom I talk to, I talk to many more who are just as friendly, but much harder to relate to. The disconnect that draws them apart so much from the rest of society is that just about all of them are true believers. They live, eat, and breathe the Dark Carnival. They alienate themselves from the rest of society and the unaffiliated, such as myself, because they see everything through Wicked Clown eyes. Violent J and Shaggy's influence touches everything in their world. When a Juggalo meets an open-minded outsider, they believe it's crucial to explain the Family's importance. Juggalos aren't proselytizers though, they just want respect from where they're coming from and are usually stoked just to talk to a listening ear. I've been treated with far more respect here than the world ever granted them. I'm not saying I haven't been met with some antagonism and distrust when a Juggalo learns I'm not a part of the Dark Carnival, but for the most part, when I tell them I'm a "punk," they think I came into that culture for the very same reason they became Juggalos. And therein lies a common understanding; we may differ in every other way, but the fact we're misfits and outcasts holds weight. Or maybe I just haven't told them enough about myself.

"You're the only one who's given us a chance," a Juggalo named Brian tells me. "Most [outsiders] just want to take us at a surface level."

This may hold true, but unlike a lot of people with counter-culture roots, me and Damon willingly admit that no matter how goofy the Juggalo aesthetic may seem to us, we come from a similar place, and maybe that makes it easier for us to understand the Juggalos. We too are familiar with shocking imagery and taking pride in being marginalized from our time spent in punk rock. We didn't listen to Psychopathic Records, but we did listen to psychopaths like GG Allin, who stabbed himself with broken glass and beat up and threw shit at his audience. And Richard Hell went onstage wearing a collared shirt with "please kill me" painted on it, wearing his inner turmoil on his sleeve. Of course, plenty of punks distinctly hate Juggalos, placing themselves on a pedestal because their culture has the propensity to be more intellectual and culturally relevant. Maybe this smugness comes from its DIY philosophy, one that worked as a springboard to radical politics, anarchism, zines/small presses, and simply dropping out and living off the grid. Maybe it's just because it's better art. But it's hard to deny the similarities between the wickedness of the Dark Carnival and the filth of punk.

I'm reminded of my train ride to Louisville to meet up with Damon. I shared a seat with young Korean guy whom I befriended. He had just spent a semester in Vancouver, Canada learning English, and spoke it well for only knowing it such a short amount of time. The two of us hung out in the lounge car with some other travelers. I talked about the Juggalos and my intentions behind attending their Gathering. I'm not sure how much he followed, as I tend to talk fast, but he understood enough to ask how someone like him, foreign with limited knowledge of American culture, would be accepted out there. At the time, I couldn't answer that question, but now I think he would be welcomed at The Gathering. Juggalos are always on the defense, because everything they care about is so reviled. But someone from a foreign culture who knows absolutely nothing about them would be just the kind of person to bring their guard down, and they'd probably feel compelled to show him a really good time.

Following the "most hated band in the world" though, is a big responsibility. A couple of Juggalos threatened to kick my ass out here after finding out I'm not a Juggalo. It was always when they were in a group and more clannish. Mostly though, the Juggalos are cool. It's the Juggalos who have a lot more going on in their lives, like Jared, that we relate to, but we've found they aren't very common.

As I've mentioned before, Insane Clown Posse lucked out and built an entire career around stuff they were into as kids, but the weird part is how the Juggalos just eat it up. Everything the ICP is down with, Juggalos obsess over. Some Juggalos lack complexity and individuality, buying the whole wicked dream. I'm hard-pressed to find a Juggalo who will say, "I love ICP, but I think Faygo is too sweet, and besides, pop is an unhealthy beverage," or "I love my Fam but honestly, I'm more of a fan of Russian literature than wrestling," or "I'm a Juggalette, but I find Faygo wet t-shirt contests to be degrading to women." No, everything trickles top-down from a couple of charismatic clown leaders, and the whole of the Juggalos follow. This level of unquestioning adherence to ICP only builds upon itself, because the more the Juggalos get behind it, the more they alienate themselves from the rest of the world and seek respite in the Family.

When talking about ICP's leadership with a friend, he suggested I read *The Spider and the Starfish*. This book describes two business models: the spider, which keeps all the control in the center of its web, and the starfish, which breaks off an arm that another starfish grows from. The starfish is like a model of business that's successful in the information age. He lists Apple as an example which, by allowing clients more access, such as free podcast hosting and using client-to-client tech support, has created a sycophantic community that does a whole lot of their promotion and work for them. Businesses that aren't adapting to this decentralized model in the Information Age are crashing and burning. DIY and underground cultures have always survived because they work on the starfish model. Punk can lead you to zine culture, which could lead you into feminism or anarchism. Hip hop can lead you into graffiti or Black Liberation struggles. But ICP has always been the spider to the Juggalos' spider web. ICP use an outdated model, but it's working. And it's baffling how well it's working.

# JUGGALO ISLAND

*On Juggalo island,*

*We can be one,*

*Let our nuts hang by the water,*

*On Juggalo island, we can have fun,*

*We can let go, by the water*

—Insane Clown Posse, "Juggalo Island"

*What we do is secret-secret!*

—The Germs

ICP recently finished shooting a video for their song "Juggalo Island" at The Gathering. Like "Miracles," ICP released "Juggalo Island" for the Juggalos, but also as an insular reply to the accidental notoriety they received for "Miracles." It's a sappy number about how great it would be if all the Juggalos inhabited their own island where they could all "be one" and just let their "nuts hang by the water," leaving the world—the rest of the world who hate them—behind. The video features footage of Juggalos making homemade waterslides, swinging off ropes into Hepatitis Lake, grilling hot dogs, and dancing. Just the Family with some Psychopathic Records rappers mixed in—no models, no celebrities, just Juggalos. Fucking unity. How does that work?

"It's every motherfucker here that makes The Gathering worth it, man. I remember the first time with, like, Juggalos, whether they're, I dunno, fucking mushroomheads, whatever, dude. It just makes it all worth it. First time, the greatest day in the world. Alright?" says a Juggalo known as Jaymo.

A lot of the Juggalos talk about The Gathering being their conversion, but for many it happened in the crowd getting hosed down with Faygo at an ICP concert. The Family is very real and valid; it's something so strong that they commit their entire lives to it.

Just like the lower rung of commerce, there seems to be a lower rung of Clown Love—one that hits on a deeper and more real level than the adoration Juggalos have for ICP and Psychopathic Records, and I really feel it in the air here.

"If I see someone wearing an ICP shirt that isn't a Juggalo, I'll tell them to take that shit off, dog, that's my Family, man. They'll be all, 'oh okay, my bad' and it's cool, but that's how I feel about it," another Juggalo tells me.

I'm starting to learn that Family strongly draws people to become a Juggalo and in the process, one picks up the Dark Carnival, not the other way around. The Dark Carnival adapts and moves fluidly, akin to how the Family accepts other Juggalos. The camaraderie of the Family makes all of it appealing: ICP, the Dark Carnival, and Wicked Shit.

It seems once a Juggalo becomes involved with the Dark Carnival, they enmesh themselves further and further into it and withdraw from the outside world. The Family replaces everything and they listen to every word ICP tells them, making information from anywhere else less and less relevant. I've heard people say the Dark Carnival sounds like a cult. I disagree. After all, no one's forcing anyone to stay, telling them to reject their other family and friends, nor, to my knowledge, shunning them if they leave. I prefer to call them cultish, because they certainly perpetuate cultish elements. For instance, the way they speak their own language and the way Family permeates their entire existence. Learning this about the Family clears up a lot of what I fail to understand in the lyrics, as Juggalos apply meaning to them after they feel Clown Love. I fail to get it because I haven't opened my mind to get it.

"It's bliss, it's like nirvana and pretty much like a version of Heaven I guess. It can be heaven depending on who you are. If you're into religion, it is heaven. It's whatever makes you happy," Fuckstick says about Clown Love.

"Everybody has their own outlook on Clown Love," Bubbles tells me. "You can't just take it from two random Juggalos."

"Honestly, you're gonna have to interview every Juggalo," Kentucky tells me, "because it's different for everyone."

•     •     •

The sun starts to go down. Damon and I are lit up on Percocet and whiskey, and heading to the Main Stage to check out '90s G-funk rapper Warren G. The crowd tallied around 15,000 last night, but right now the crowd is sparse. The Juggalos keep themselves busy by throwing trash all over the place. Damon and I laugh as the trash flies all around, pelting us. Ahead, a backyard-style wrestling Battle Royale breaks out—ninjas just start beating each other with folding chairs and whatever else they find. I pull a Juggalo aside for a photo. He wears a Hatchet Gear hockey jersey embroidered with a dark, faceless, hooded figure with the words "The Wraith" emblazoned across the back. An open gash drips blood on his forehead, and he flashes the devil sign and sticks out his tongue for the picture. We giddily take pictures of the Juggalos acting the most outrageous in their clown make up, and they gladly ham it up for the camera. We put ourselves in the pictures with them, and they throw up Wicked Clown hand signs. Juggalos love having their pictures taken. It's funny though, because these photos won't be used for my book—no, the pictures document the trip for ourselves. And right now, we are having one hell of a time.

"How long has it been since Warren G played a show?" I wonder, as I dodge Faygo bottles, punch giant beach balls flying toward me, and realize I'm actually enjoying the worst mainstream rapper of the '90s...I mean, I fucking hate Warren G.

"Hey ninja, I like that Crass tattoo," a tall, muscular, Latino Juggalo says, pointing to Damon's shoulder. "I love that band."

It's the first time we cross an actual cultural divide between the Juggalos and us. Crass was a radical anarchist band from the '70s in England. Revolutionary and completely anti-state to the point of irritating arrogance, they are most famous for radicalizing and politicizing several generations of young people, and promoting communalism and revolution.

The crossover into familiar territory shocks me, and I wish I could take the ninja aside and ask him why he likes the band, how he discovered them, and how it pertains to being a Juggalo. But I'm too fucked up, so I say nothing while Damon makes small talk with him. Then I forget about it completely, when I'm struck on the shoulder with a near full can of beer.

"That was a full can of beer!" I shout to Damon, offended at the waste of alcohol. The punks would never waste a perfectly good beer.

"Get over it," Damon says. And I stop thinking of such things.

# EMBRACES

*A knife in my hand and I know what I expect of me,*

*The blood lust in the fear is what I'm lookin' for,*

*Rush in my veins as I rush and slowly bleed this whore,*

*It's pure desire and it burns at me like fire,*

*Mercedes and a murder spree is what it takes to get me higher*

— Boondox, "Rollin' Hard" Psychopathic Records
Artist

*Carnival don't fuck around,*

*Fire up the tilt-a-whirl,*

*And we'll see you all in hell,*

*They all die,*

*They All Die,*

*Round and round and round you go,*

*Yo, the dark carnival will never die.*

— Insane Clown Posse, "Tilt-A-Whirl"

Darkness is setting in when we decide to ride the Tilt-A-Whirl. We stand in line behind a chubby girl with a tattoo in the middle of her back, the inscription "Skrilla" on a banner sandwiched between two Hatchetmen. I ask to take a picture and she lets me, the flash bringing out the sunburn on her back. I have a moment of clarity as I look at the picture on my camera screen—the disembodied skin of a person whose Clown name may or may not be Skrilla. I'm uncomfortable with taking it, and put the camera away for a while. We get on the ride and a Juggalette turns from her seat in front of me and says,

"What's up, 'lo?"

She's pretty with long blonde hair. On her forearm is a stylish tattoo of an old-style compass one might see on a treasure map, and around her neck she wears a leather bondage choker with long loops hanging from it.

"Are you enjoying the Gathering?" she asks.

"Yeah, I'm having a really good time," I say as things start spinning.

She tells me her name and the location of a party her camp is throwing tonight, but both slip my mind. The ride stops and Damon and I stumble dizzily off it towards each other, the drugs and booze all twisted up in our stomachs. Damon tells me he'll meet me back at the van and wanders off to puke his guts out. Determined to press on, I head to the Midway and buy a corn dog to settle my own queasiness. It does the job and, fully recovered, I head to the Drug Bridge to mingle.

I dodge golf carts and golf carts narrowly dodge me. "*Whoop! Whoop!*" Juggalos from the carts shout, and I laugh and yell it back to them. Now that the sun is down and Psychopathic bands are about to go on, more and more 'lo's and 'lettes paint themselves up. The evil grins fit the party atmosphere.

I pass one of the carnival games. A Juggalo and a carny stand in front of a dunking tank. On the dunking tank sits a topless woman, and the two men haggle over the price of the balls needed to throw to dunk the girl.

"Can I take her out to Hepatitis Lake with me if I win?" the Juggalo asks.

"Yeah, sure, sure, you can take her."

"Uh uh! No!" the girl shouts from her place on the tank.

Life fills Drug Bridge. Dealers holler out what they're peddlin'. Buyers barter. A pear-shaped Juggalette offers titty-flashes to sweeten the deal on a dub sack. Deals are made everywhere so everyone can roll, trip, or get high for the show. Juggalos pass by holding handmade signs of the drugs they're selling. I'm sitting with Kentucky just shooting the shit. I genuinely like Kentucky, his energy and enthusiasm, and since this is his house I let him do most of the talking. He's a lot younger than me and I wonder how his life's going to unfold; I hope the best for him and every Juggalo out here. Directly across from us, leaning on the opposite rail, a short guy holds his own large sign that proclaims, "I just wanted to waste your time."

"What do you think of '*Whoop! Whoop!*'?" Kentucky asks me.

"Well, I think it's kind of goofy but it seems to have its purpose. Ya know? For instance, those times when everybody's partying and some dude comes up to you all fucked up and babbling and shouting, or whatever. He's just having a good time, but you don't know what to say? Well, you can just say *Whoop! Whoop!* You know? Times like that."

"Yeah, I know what you're saying," Kentucky laughs.

Connecting with Kentucky is easy. I think humanizing someone throws a rope-a-dope to your ego. So often enough we avoid it like a disease, but if it happens it's really not so bad. It's calming even, to strip down your arrogance, leaving only the bare essence of what makes us human. It brings people around to the facts we all struggle and life is damned hard. I think about my own shortcomings. I'm fucked up, my mind awash in pills and booze to calm all my self-doubt about jumping into this project, about chucking all journalistic integrity out the window. As I chill with Kentucky, I think of others I've met out here. Not everybody (hell, I've found plenty of fucking dumbshits out here), but everybody who's cool, who respected me. And I wonder what the true nature of betrayal is. Is it intent or lack of honesty?

A guy in a tie-dye shirt with long, gray, balding hair wanders across the Drug Bridge. He's gazing wall-eyed at everything around him, tripping balls.

"Hey, what's up?" Kentucky asks him.

He gives a dazed smile and a slow languorous wave. Kentucky says, *"Whoop! Whoop!"*

"That old dude's fucked up," I say.

"That's Gallagher," Kentucky tells me, the '70s comedian famous for taking sledgehammers to watermelons.

"Chase him down and I'll get a picture of you with him," I tell Kentucky.

He does, and I snap the picture: Kentucky with a big grin and his arm around Gallagher, frying on acid. Then I head back to camp to catch up to Damon and re-up on booze. He's chilling around the van shooting the shit with some Juggalos and drinking whiskey.

"Hey, I was hoping you'd make it back. That ride made me puke five times."

"This is Craven," he tells the 'los he's chilling with.

I flop down and smile to myself. I'm having a hell of a time; I'm with my best friend and 20,000 Juggalos in the middle of nowhere and I'm about to listen to clowns rap. I'm not sure any of this counts as journalism, but I'll be damned if I care right now.

•　　　•　　　•

The sun's gone down on all our drinking. Boondox, Psychopathic Records' backwoods, white-boy rapper, plays onstage, his face clowned up in black and white. From the edges of his greasepaint, a jagged smile curves like a jack-o-lantern done in a tribal tattoo design. He rocks a cowboy hat and flannel, pointing his finger-gun into the crowd. The Juggalos throw theirs back up at him. "*Whoop! Whoop!*" they all yell. He kicks rhymes about moonshine and taking Ecstasy and stabbing, hacking up, and asphyxiating anybody who fucks with him or Psychopathic.

Or just anybody, period. *"Whoop! Whoop!"* yells the crowd. And the booze, the pills, and the Clown Love all kick in. I slide into the visceral night and start getting down. Damon and I shout along with the crowd. *"Whoop! Whoop!"* Wicked clowns pass us joints. Faygo bottles, beer cans, and all other projectiles fly about. Titties bounce this way and that. Just about everybody is rolling, tripping, or in some other way fucked the hell up! Total freedom! Nobody looks twice at Damon or me, and for all they know we're just down-ass 'los. And I don't know about you, but I don't want to be on my deathbed knowing I missed a chance to party with some folks just because they dressed like a bunch of clowns.

*"Fam-uh-lee! Fam-uh-lee! Fam-uh-lee!"* The crowd chants as Boondox, his hype man, and the rest of the crowd leave the stage. My stomach flutters with pill buzz and humanity as I talk to Nick, a ninja with long, unkempt, brown hair from Boulder.

"I just think this is wonderful what you guys have. We just came out here to check it out but we're having a great time. I think it's incredible how you guys have this Family and stuff," I rave uncontrollably.

"We all take care of each other," he says. "It doesn't matter who you are or where you're from. If you're down with the Hatchet then you're family."

I may be leading the witnesses in my quest to figure out what the Juggalos are all about, but Juggalos I've talked with all say the same thing about the Family. None of them had anything before the Dark Carnival. Nothing since has matched this feeling of freedom, unity, and love. They're down for life, hooked on the connection they feel. The Juggalo from Boulder gives me a hug. Now I get it. The Family doesn't question, or pull rank, or cut itself into subgenres. It doesn't mire itself in politics or lack of politics. It's just freedom, man. For all my participation in underground subcultures, I've never felt anything like this. It's more than a concert where you "feel the love in the room," and afterward everyone goes on with their lives. For the Juggalos, the Family realness lasts.

As the night progresses, I slip even more into the Clown Love. Titties flash everywhere throughout the night. The *"fam-uh-lee!"* chant never stops. Hands pass out drugs and booze everywhere. More backyard wrestling matches commence— flashlight wrestling matches and midget wrestling leagues. There are no narcs or security, and nothing to stop the non-stop hedonism except for other 'los, and that only happens when someone really fucks up. *Fam-uh-lee!!*

"Ketamine," I yell at some point on the Drug Bridge. "Does anybody have Ketamine?"

"Ketamine?" A thick Juggalette comes up to me. "You have Ketamine?"

"No, I was looking for it…"

"Aw, fuck," she says, visibly bummed.

"Me too," I say. "Well, how about a hug?"

"Sure," she says, and embraces me as Damon laughs over my shoulder.

I just hugged a Juggalette… *I just hugged a Juggalette!!*

As the hours of my conversion slide quickly by, I watch Kottonmouth Kings rap about weed and I see Violent J's cryptic spiritual band, The Dark Lotus, kick the knowledge. I vaguely recollect seeing some Juggalette rapping about weed and fucking people up, and I remember some fat guys making fun of me and moving on to another set of clown faces to bro down with.

As the night goes on, things fade in and out. I lose and find Damon as we wander drunkenly through the Dark Carnival. I miss Lil' Kim, but see a very baked Tom Green get the crowd to repeatedly chant "chicken sandwich" before I feel antsy and leave. I see Gallagher several more times wandering around, frying on acid. I lose hours and hours I have no recollection of. I regret it later as bad journalism, but if my intention was to get down like the 'los do, well I guess I'm doing it. All I say to each Juggalo I meet is that I think they're great and the Family is one of the greatest things I've ever experienced.

In and out of rolling blackouts. Gentle ninja hands and arms grab me out of the darkness.

"Hey ninja, are you okay? Do you need some water?" they ask.

Further down other 'los check up on me. Clown Love.

Near the van, but not quite ready to fall out, I wander to other camps nearby and bro down. I chat to a 'lo named Gore from Kansas. He sits around a gas camp stove, cooking a pan of ramen. He's about 18 and appears glad to talk to me.

"You want some?" he says, leaning toward me with the pan.

"No, thanks," I say, and we continue to talk for a while.

"Yeah, most of us came from fucked up places, man. Never had families or had kind-of fucked up families. The Dark Carnival, this is our Family. This is why we're here."

"Before I got here…I'd read that Juggalos come from all sorts of… are widely… diverse. But so far it seems like you're all pretty poor folks, working class folks… You get what I'm… saying… "

"None of us have any money, ninja," Gore says seriously.

A couple of Juggalos and a Juggalette argue nearby. Something about somebody throwing something at someone else. I'm not really paying attention. It's none of my business and sounds like some drunk bullshit to me.

"It's like tonight, man, some shit went down," he pauses, waving his fork at his arguing camp crew. "It's not perfect, but this is where the love is, man."

# TITTIES AND BRICKS: RELATION AND ASSIMILATION

*Oooh (Areola!), Oooh (Areola!), Oooh (Areola!)*

*That shirt came off and showed a...*

*Oooh (Areola!), Oooh (Areola!)*

> — Tech N9ne and 816 Boys, "Areola"

*Smack that bitch right across the lips,*

*'cause she ain't nothin' but a filthy bitch,*

*beat the freak in the head with a cinder block,*

*blacken her eyes your lunatic tock...*

> — Insane Clown Posse, "Dear ICP"

162 · Juggalo Country ∭

How I managed to recover so well from last night's indulgent bacchanal, I have no idea. It's almost noon, and Damon and I have been camped out at Lake Hepatitis. Far too hot to sleep after the sun started to rise, we've been getting in and out of the grimy water all morning, the only escape from another sweltering day. The Juggalos strip the dock of the plastic barrels underneath, which keep it afloat. It's tethered to the bottom of Hepatitis Lake by a very long rope. With fewer and fewer barrels holding it up, the dock is mostly submerged under water except for whichever corner is butting up, ballasted (or anti-ballasted) by whatever side the more obese Juggalos stand on.

Plastic bottles fly all about. When we get in the water we keep a constant eye out for bottles thrown by the beach 'los as the dock lurks around us under the water. If we're not looking, a sunken corner of it will scoop us up.

"Heads up, ninja!" says a Juggalo near us to his buddy.

Not paying attention, a very fat, shirtless, tattooed Juggalo gets nailed right in the head with a gallon-sized Faygo bottle. The bottle contains a mixture of lake water and the remains of the soda.

"Aw shit, I yelled 'heads up,' man. You okay?" his friend says.

Without blinking an eye, he picks up the bottle and chugs from it.

"Man, I just don't give a fuck. I just want to fuck a bitch with AIDS so I can get skinny and die," he says after a swig.

Sitting on my towel, I jot the following quotes down in my journal:

"I'm going to waggle my dick in his eye."

Juggalette: "Have you ever had sex on videotape for money?"

Juggalo: "Well, not for money."

"I sprinkled some mushroom powder on my spaghetti when I was at my grandma's and almost lost my shit. It sucked, ninja."

"Blacky! Blacky! Black guy! Hey, black!"

"I have Faygo titty and everybody want to see it."

"I'm keeping close track of all of the crazy shit that I hear people say out here," I tell Damon.

Out in the water, a shirtless Juggalo in mirrored sunglasses rides a blue barrel floating in the water.

"Johnny Knoxville, I'm Johnny Knoxville," he shouts, arms and legs wrapped around the barrel as it bobs up and down.

"Did you write down, 'How about a hug?'" Damon says, mocking me for my Ketamine hug last night.

"Fuck you," I say back.

"Well, I paid five dollars to see a girl's titties last night," he says. "I guess that was my own version of the K hug."

He goes on to tell the story.

"So I was trying to chat this girl up. I was all 'hey, what's your name, I want to get to know you… or whatever and she says, 'you want to see my titties don't you' So I said, 'yeah, yeah, I do want to see your titties.' So she said, 'well I'll show you my titties if you buy my friends glow sticks.' They're two for five bucks. So I did. That was my last five bucks."

Damon likes to consider himself "pro-sleaze." What he calls pro-sleaze, I tend to call sexism—a disarming and childish sort of sexism. Then again, we all find ways to get around questioning our friends sometimes (and by proxy, ourselves). Damon revels in all the skin and flesh of The Gathering and I waver between ethical distance and journalistic immersion. I feel a bit of complicity, which I excuse in the name of new journalism. There's also nobody looking over our shoulders here, and we've taken advantage of that. Nevertheless, we at least know how to act.

Titties are some of the most important attractions, commodities, and subjects at The Gathering. The chant of "*Titties! Tit-ties!*" constantly resounds the air. The 'los display signs at their camps saying, "free shots for tits." Juggalos walk around with signs asking to see titties. Juggalettes carry around signs saying things like "See my tits: ~~$5.00~~ ~~$4.00~~ $3.00." The lack of class and floobiness in these actions reveal much about the lack of empowerment, not only with 'lettes, but within the subculture itself.

Another thing Damon and I notice is that after 'los request, shout, or barter for titty flashes, the 'lettes put them away and both parties move on. Very little flirtation or Juggalos kicking game occurs. The Juggalos act pretty awkward and shy around the 'lettes, and perhaps that's why they settle for just gawking at boobies for a few seconds. Maybe the mating habits of Juggalos are more complex and I'm just not picking up on them, but from my distance the Juggalos present themselves as a bit shy and lacking in social skills, even when totally surrounded by their own people. Although Psychopathic imagery is hard and tough and violent, a lot of Juggalos just appear to be nerdy kids in evil paint.

Juggalos in relationships with 'lettes treat their partners noticeably well, often putting them on a pedestal. We've seen 'los actually carry their 'lettes into the green waters of Lake Hepatitis. They canoodle and sit apart from the rest of their group of 'los so their 'lettes get all of their attention. The Juggalos we see hooked-up also tend to be in their late 20s and 30s, and appear to have been together for a long time. So the Juggalettes are either disrespected as objects, or treated with knightly chivalry when partnered up. The most revealing thing about a culture, a faith, or a group of people of any sort is how they treat and respect women, and the way women demand respect within that milieu. It says something about the balance of power. A good example in my world are the Riot Grrrl and Queercore movements, where women and queer-identifying people stood up to the straight male dominance in punk, forcing their scenes to hear and recognize them.

There might be room in the future for these demands in Juggalo culture. Because while The Gathering's titty commodity is blatantly sexist—in sync with so much else that's misogynistic about Wicked Shit and Juggalo culture—the Juggalos, being the misfits they are, leave a backdoor open for body positivity. It's really kind of sweet. Most of this sentiment comes from the "if you're Fam, you're Fam" philosophy. So a Juggalette is attractive simply because they're a Juggalette. The idea of floob pride fits here, pride in being an outcast and an underdog. Fat girls jump at the chance to grind a pole and get positive reinforcement. Some ICP lyrics show love to the fat girls. Underneath it all lies an honest resistance to unnatural and unfair beauty standards.

·     ·     ·

"Hey, what's up?" Richie says, shirtless and dressed in swim trunks.

"Oh, hi, good morning," Damon replies. "I was just busting Craven here's balls because he gave a girl a Ketamine hug last night."

Richie looks puzzled. So he tells him the story and Richie chuckles.

"I heard Tila Tequila got a brick thrown at her last night," he says.

This is the first we hear of the attack. He tells us Tom Green jumped to her defense and got beat down, too. I immediately regret missing this juicy event, as I wandered around fucked-up and acting a fool the night before.

"Where in the hell is someone going to get a brick out here?" asks Damon, gesturing to the lake, the field, the trees.

"I may be a jackass, but y'all busted my lip open," yells the Juggalo imitating Johnny Knoxville from the lake; someone just hit him with a rock during the bottle fight.

"Not cool," he mutters, climbing back onto his barrel as the trash continues flying with nobody really listening to him..

For all the talk about the Tila Tequila incident, we meet few Juggalos who actually saw anything. I realize that's what the big argument last night at Gore's camp was about—not inner-camp conflict. The upset 'lette chewed out her 'lo for being in on the Tila attack.

"This is where the story is," Damon says looking at the program.

Yeah, and I had every opportunity to watch it last night, but instead I just ran around partying with Juggalos everywhere *but* the second stage. Floob.

"Hey, look," Damon says. Holding the program, he points to a picture of Tila's face.

"Brick!" he says, and we laugh.

As the day progresses we hear more and more rumors of the attack, each far more outrageous than the last. I'm still afraid to just come out and ask someone exactly who the hell Tila Tequila is! Since everybody here seems to know, I just assume I'm supposed to know, too. I don't want to out myself as a non-Juggalo by revealing my ignorance. I was unaware that I should know Tila Tequila, not because I hadn't done enough research on Wicked Shit, but instead because she's a D-list celebrity. And it turns out, I do know Tila Tequila; I just haven't realized it yet. I caught clips of her show, *A Shot of Love with Tila Tequila*, in some bar or waiting room. Tequila, a media whore along the lines of Paris Hilton, is pretty much famous for being famous. A 4' 11" model with giant fake breasts, Tila appeared in *Playboy* at age 18, and from there used sleaze to climb ladders until she landed a show on which a bunch of brain-dead douchebags competed to date her. It was enough to make her a minor celebrity, and with the help of some domestic disputes and controversy, she became a bit of a spectacle in the media. I thought it'd hurt my street cred to ask the Juggalos who she was, but apparently it's pretty hard not to know. And this highlights the Juggalos' problem with her. They find her insulting to their gathering, feel she is here to exploit them, and that she has no business at their underground, horrorcore rap festival. And they made sure she knew.

Me and Damon weren't the only ones naive to Tila. After the attack, ICP told the media they didn't even know her. They claimed the organizers only told them about a "hot bitch" who raps, and they gave the go ahead. Tila Tequila and Insane Clown Posse both used negative attention to get where they are—the more controversy they get, the more people pay attention to them. It wouldn't surprise me if both sides went into this hoping for a spectacle, allowing Tila to stretch out her 15 minutes, and Insane Clown Posse to throw out another net to catch negative press.

More information comes our way. We learn Tila wasn't pelted with a brick, but with rocks—a whole lot of them. To make things worse, people also threw bottles of piss and feces at her. We even hear tell of a watermelon soaked in a porta-potty all day being chucked at her. The crowd demanded she take her top off, shouting "show us your tits." She complied with this command while taunting the crowd, shouting "I ain't going anywhere."

A few wrestlers guarded her from the onslaught, finally dragging her off the stage against her will. At that point things completely exploded. A mob of Juggalos chased her and her by-proxy bodyguards to her trailer and busted out the windows.

The part about Tom Green, however, wasn't true; he just ran out onto the runway and did a stupid dance to de-escalate things. Nobody fucked with him. The Juggalos like Tom Green, but they see right through Tila, and maybe even to some degree (against my initial assumption) Insane Clown Posse.

"It's more commercialized bullshit they're trying to bring in here, 'cause it seems like ICP is getting more and more commercialized," a Juggalo named Bill tells me.

"Man, it's part of a conspiracy to make Insane Clown Posse more mainstream," his buddy says, backing him up. "They've been doing this shit for a while. Like, they [Violent J and Shaggy] were on *Aqua Teen Hunger Force* and *Squidbillies* making fun of Juggalos."

He's referring to Cartoon Network's "Adult Swim," a programming block of absurdist and ironic cartoons popular with college kids and stoners. My friends keep sending me the clips of the episodes with Juggalo parodies, and from what I've seen, they poke fun at the Family, not ICP.

"I've seen those," I say. "I didn't know that ICP was involved."

"You could tell it was their voices," he says with disappointed distaste.

A lot of Juggalos feel the Family has a bad enough reputation without adding in more bad press. Attacking a woman goes against what a lot of Juggalos feel is Family morality. They're also worried about how it will play-out in the press—affecting their already bad reputation. Older Juggalos, disappointed by the violence, shame the declining ethics of younger Family members who don't understand the core meaning of the Family. Still, most of them feel little sympathy for the banal pop star who took shit and piss to the face.

"I would've left if I was there seeing it happen, but I was asleep. I wouldn't have participated 'cause that's just wrong in general," a Juggalo named Chris tells me.

"It was funny. It was fucked up, but it was funny. It shouldn't have happened. She just shouldn't be here, that's all," another says.

Damon and I take it with a bit of humor, too. A wealthy Hollywood dirtbag getting pelted with piss and shit amuses us too. Do we wish it hadn't happened? Well, I guess nobody deserves to get rocks thrown at them, but like most of the Juggalos we find it morbidly funny. I carry about as much sympathy for her as I would any other richie... Tom Cruise... Paris Hilton... Bret Michaels. Hell, I'd laugh if any of them got pelted with shit and rocks. I view them all as enemies of the people. Coming up in punk, we also hold the mainstream in contempt—for the wealth, power, and spectacle. We come at it from different angles, but the Juggalos and punks both despise mainstream culture for similar reasons. The Juggalos want to stay raw and wicked and don't need mainstream attention. What the mainstream Tila represents insults them, and they see her as another "richie," another one of the beautiful people, another insult to their lives of struggle. But this time she entered their house, their turf, and stomped arrogantly through the one place on earth they hold sacred. They rose to protect their community, and I respect this. It may be a wild and rash grab at empowerment, and a taking control of their lives to protect what they hold dear. Misguided as it was, the attack was an act of resistance to assimilation and co-optation.

Last night, the Juggalos proved they were a force to be reckoned with. They may not all agree it was the right thing to do, but at least a thousand or so formed an unorganized attack on a moronic, failing reality-TV star. I once heard Ice-T say of The Gathering, "If this shit were political they'd shut it down." But what if Juggalos struck out against their own leaders, their own prophets, their own idols? The heroes who sell them overpriced trinkets and sate them with autographs? What if they took control? What if they turned on the "richies" in their own community, rather than a four-foot bimbo with breast implants?

I maintain a certain level of respect for the detachment Juggalos exhibit for things outside of the Dark Carnival. I appreciate this, because underneath lies the sign of a true community, one that rises up to defend itself. I came out here to try and understand this essence of the Family, and last night I understood. At the same time the Juggalos attacked Tila Tequila, I got down with the Clown. I felt the solidarity, the gory pastoral nature of The Gathering... Clown Love. This is the Kingdom of Heaven. Step Correct.

# JUGGALOS, INSANE CLOWN POSSE, AND VIOLENCE

*My axe is my buddy, we right planets wrongs,*

*Me and my ax leave bigots,*

*dead on richie's lawns,*

*My ax is my buddy, he never make me cry,*

*Me and my ax will leave a divot for your eye*

                  – Insane Clown Posse, "My Axe"

The Bomb Tent stands almost completely empty for Juggalo MC Karaoke, an event where 'los give CDs of their recordings to a stagehand who plays them. Then they rap over their own voices and beats. The few Juggalos in the tent pay little attention to the 'lo on stage, waiting their own turn to rap. Each Juggalo who gets up raps breathlessly, falling behind their own recorded voices. Most of the rappers' lyrics seem to add up to "don't fuck with me," as one skinny 'lo after another takes their turn.

"You fucking suck," says a voice amplified by a bullhorn from a golf cart packed with ninjas.

They heckle each rapper who gets onstage. A painted-up Juggalo takes a plastic bottle to the face when he raps. He gets really pissed off and starts ranting about how fucked up it is and how they're a bunch of Juffalos for throwing shit.

"Yeah, you were okay not really," the heckler with the bullhorn mocks.

The rapper storms off and at that, the stage-hand mumbles something like "all right, I'll see all of you clowns later," and just takes off.

"Do you want to hear my comedy set?" says one of the guys in the golf cart to the even emptier tent.

"Sure," someone says, and he gets up on the stage and starts his comedy set—which is just him insulting everyone.

"Hey fat-ass, you got a watermelon under that shirt?" he says to a hefty Juggalo, who cusses back at the comedian. He and his ninjas storm out of the tent.

"Fuck you," they say.

"Yeah, your girlfriend looks like she has hepatitis," he says to the backs of their heads.

"Look at this guy, with his glasses and his notebook," he says, pointing me out.

"He's a nerd," replies one of his homies in the cart.

"Yeah, but he's staying for my set, so he's cool."

He insults a few more in the tent. He's clearly not stopping until somebody makes him.

It comes back around to me,

"And yeah, fuck him for writing through my set."

Oddly, he doesn't say anything else as I walk out of the tent.

I walk back to the van, nauseated and wishing for a place to hide from the heat. Damon hangs out with Jared, drinking cold beer from the cooler. Jared drags off a blunt, adding to the already thick air. He tells us about the time a few years ago when a carjacker jumped in his car at a red light. His first impulse was to push the gun down and away from him, and it fired.

"The gun went off and shattered my leg. My leg was completely destroyed. I was housebound for three years. I mean, I could get around in a wheelchair, but it was fucking hard as hell to do. So I just went to school online and got my degree. I was able to get a scholarship because of what happened to me," he says, blowing grapey smoke into the air.

He continues to tell us about how his ex-girlfriend emptied his house of anything valuable and his bank account of all his money while he was laid up in the hospital, but he seems to make the best of it.

When Juggalos like Kentucky talk about how the violence in Wicked Shit acts as a catalyst for a healthy release of anger and aggression, it's true. But it doesn't always work out that way—sometimes violence manifests in worse ways than just throwing rocks and shit at a D-list celebrity. Murders happen in the name of the Hatchet. A quick Google search shows quite a few grisly crimes committed by Juggalos (and actually, I'll go ahead and say 'self-described Juggalos,' because most Juggalos dismiss them as Juffalos, and I'm in no place to decide who is a real Juggalo).

Take for example the grisly case of Syko Sam. Robert McCroskey, aka Syko Sam, a 20-year-old horrorcore rapper, killed four people in the small town of Farmville, Virginia. First he bludgeoned his 16-year-old girlfriend, Emma Neiderbrock, and her 18-year-old friend, Melanie Wells, to death with a hammer and a maul. Then he waited around Emma's house until her father, Pastor Marl Neiderbrock, and his estranged wife, Dr. Debra Kelley, came home and killed them in the same manner.

It reminds me of the disgust a writing peer and friend of mine once showed for the Juggalos, her attention drawn to them after I began talking about this project.

"I saw a Juggalo walking with a much smaller, much younger girl. He had all that clown makeup on and they were just walking down the street. It pissed me off. I just wanted to save her."

It's not surprising to hear her say that. She's a different kind of writer than me in a lot of ways—a romantic. Her zines possess a dignified observance of beauty, even when writing about tragedies, like deaths of friends or humanity's destruction of the earth. Her voice comes from a place of the sublime.

"They're not even human," she said of the Juggalos, only half-joking, after telling her story of seeing them on the street.

She hates what Juggalos stand for, and everything about them, but mostly the violence gets to her.

"Why are they so violent?" she asks.

For a lot of Juggalos, they were raised around violence and know it all too well. In the corners and margins of America, from the ghettos to the trailer parks, society completely stripped the underclass of culture, heritage, and dignity, and with it their sense of identity. The only trait passed down to them is violence. They are born on the receiving end of this violence. Whether the violence takes the active or passive route, whether turned inward with alcoholism or meth addictions, or cast back out into their environment through incest and spousal abuse. The poor know the language of violence well. Songs about whimsical rape and mutilation by clown characters add a level of play to this violence and flips it. People stand back and to look and laugh at it. When Juggalos take on clown names like Bloodshed or Stabbo or Ripper, they own it through the Dark Carnival. They find room to process a very real violence through abstract satire. It appears base and low-class to non-Juggalos, a sentiment which only feeds their loyalty. This violence may be hard for the outsider to understand, but for the Juggalos, it is their birthright.

•       •       •

*I don't beat women, fuck that/I'm above it/*

*but I'll cut her fucking neck and think nothing of it.*

–Insane Clown Posse, "Boogie Woogie Wu"

"We did horrible things," Violent J says of his and Shaggy's thugging days in *Behind the Paint*. "There were these hookers who used to hang out in front of this motorcycle club called the Iron Coffins, and we'd call them over like we were going to pick them up. Right when they'd lean over into the window, we'd whip bricks at their faces like, 'bitch, get the hell out of here.' We would leave them lying bloody in the street. I can't believe we actually did that shit, now."

As sadistic as this sounds, at least Violent J refers to it as something he's moved on from. He seems repentant of it, if not regretful. For this reason alone, I find the boastful tone he takes on later, when bragging about beating the shit out of audience members, more repulsive. Particularly so when a crowd-surfer flipped them off, and they beat him with a mic stand to the point where he ended up in the hospital. When some Juggalos came forward as witnesses, ICP dismissed them as fake Juggalos just like they quickly dismiss Juggalos like Syko Sam who commit senseless murder. Beating the shit out of an audience member who throws up an insulting gesture may be less horrific than bludgeoning four people to death, but both acts require a lack of impulse control. Both acts are egocentric; Syko Sam acted to get revenge on the world and make people submit to his will. For ICP, they act because they believe God blessed them, because they are above criticism, and they want ninjas to submit to their will. I believe ICP tends to make moral judgments according to how actions and outcomes benefit them. Being associated with Syko Sam reflects badly upon them, and letting a guy get away with flipping them off wounds their ego and makes them appear weak. They responded in accordance to their beliefs in each situation.

I think the title Psychopathic Records gives away more than ICP intends. They seem to take no responsibility and show little remorse for their own violence, while at the same time teaching morality, however warped, to their followers.

Even ICP's lyrics to their songs, which they claim are moral tales, elicit confusion. Plenty of the Wicked Clown victims in the songs aren't rich or wife-beaters. They constantly flip back and forth in their justification of violence. When it's against innocents, such as a cat or a woman, they consider the violence a fantasy. When it's against kid diddlers and wife-beaters, the violence is warranted. They fall into the basic trappings of faith—by being blessed with the Dark Carnival prophecy, they seem to think they only act correctly. They fail to see their own actions and lifestyles as hypocritical to their message. I could chalk it up to male privilege or wealth, but ICP seems to remain completely obtuse to their own actions. Psychopathic.

·        ·        ·

Damon and I sweat it out in the Freakshow Tent. Flec's Circus Sideshow performs on the stage. We just watched a guy breathe fire, a woman do some hula-hoop tricks, and a pretty impressive display of contact juggling. A guy with an "octo-bong"—a beer bong with five hoses and a collapsible stand that extends several feet to accommodate the chuggers from a standing position—mills about the tent. Standing near us is a white kid, his braided hair tied with multi-colored rubber bands. He can't be more than fifteen. He wears a t-shirt that says "Juggalo, Porch Monkey For Life" on the back, a crude misunderstanding of an already controversial joke from the movie *Clerks 2*.

Crew members unload a huge rubber ring with "Slick Chix" written on the side into the tent and machine-inflate it in just a few minutes. The M.C and owner of Slick Chix starts announcing the beginning of Ladies' Oil Wrestling. He's got that short, spiky haircut with frosted tips that's popular with schmucks. My brain fails to recall his name in the heat, so let's just call him Dick Macken. Dick Macken starts by telling everyone not to throw shit during the event or he'll shut it down. He also says cable television will air the event later (on a station focusing on video games), and the Juggalos "*Whoop! Whoop!*"

He instructs, "Before we get started, I want everyone to shout with me, '*Fuck girls gone wild!*' Say it for the camera, this is going to be on television, *say it loud for the camera!* '*Fuck girls gone wild!*'"

"*Fuck girls gone wild!*" the Juggalos chant as more and more of them crowd gathers around the ring.

"*Fuck girls gone wild!*" Dick leads.

"*Fuck girls gone wild!*" the Juggalos chant back.

Eventually, some girls wearing Slick Chix swimsuits climb into the ring. Dick reminds the Juggalos he'll shut it down if they throw shit, and announces the names of the two wrestlers.

"Now," he says, "we come to a favorite part of the show for the Juggalos that I like to call 'Oiling Down the Bitch.'"

He grabs two teen 'los out of the audience and hands each of them a bottle of baby oil, which they start spraying on the Slick Chix.

"No, no that's not how you do it," he says and takes the bottle back. "This is how you do it."

He spreads the girl's legs apart and holds the bottle to his crotch, makes some orgasm-simulating grunts, and squirts oil all over the girl. He gives the bottle back to the Juggalo who, with a hint of awkwardness, follows suit. Teenage Juggalos crowd around the wrestler, smacking her ass. She smiles and writhes as the oil cascades over her, soaking her. Uncomfortable, I scan the crowd and see a Juggalo near me holding his five-year-old Juggalette daughter on his shoulders.

After a few rounds of frosted Dick's girls wrestling, he starts pulling Juggalettes from the crowd to compete. In this particular match, the first one to rip the bikini off the other Juggalette declares victory.

"Our first contestant is… " He holds the microphone to the very young 'lette.

"Tammy," she says.

"Do you have a boyfriend?" Macken asks.

"No."

"Do you want one?" he says, then seeming to forget where he is and what he's doing, tells her over the mic, "Go to my website, [dick-macken]-dot-com. You'll see how much money I make."

Then he remembers he's announcing an event and turns to the crowd.

"Uh, you guys all check it out too [dick-macken]-dot-com."

The wrestlers start ripping each other's clothes off and rolling in the oil. The sweaty Juggalos press tightly around the ring for a view, while the 'los behind them curve their heads up-and-over and side-to-side to get a glimpse. I join in but never get a view of the ring, and when I catch myself straining around the Juggalos for a better view, I tell Damon I've had enough. I'm hot, sticky, offended, aroused, and wondering how many people I know might stumble upon a cable channel focusing on video games. I see Nathan and Samantha, the Portland couple, in the crowd as I walk from the tent. We smile at each other and shrug.

# JUGGALOS AND THE LGBTQ COMMUNITY

*That night when I got back from my first walk in years and years, I didn't reach for those chips. I said to myself, "Those are faggot chips. For every chip I eat a homo gets to grab my balls."*

— Violent J on dieting, *ICP: Behind the Paint*

*Fuck Forrest Gump/he probably takes it in the rump*

— Insane Clown Posse, "Fuck the World"

"Yo, you all caressing my hand 'n' shit," Adam, a shirtless white Juggalo in Hatchet Gear basketball shorts, says loudly, cutting his interview short by jerking his hand back from my handshake and storming off offended. He acted really cool before that, talking about what the Family and the Dark Carnival meant to him.

"No wait…" I say, somewhat taken aback and confused.

"Nah, dog, you were caressin' my hand 'n' shit," he repeats and stomps out of Spazzmatic.

"Don't worry about him," his homie, James, a chubby 'lo of sixteen, says. "He's just really drunk."

James, still curious about my attempts at getting the Juggalo story, and wanting to tell his, apologizes for his friend's behavior and tries to make up for it. I keep recording and feign interest, but in my mind I try to process what just happened. Adam's problem with my "caressin'" handshake probably comes from Violent J's frequent complaints about "feeble" and "ginger-ass" handshakes. For instance, Violent J complains in his book about how all the wrestlers he's met shake hands in a wimpy way. It's a pet peeve of his. Adam is influenced by J's alpha-male handshake predisposition enough to question my masculinity and sexuality (or maybe his own sexuality). Maybe I make some assumptions here. Maybe he's never heard Violent J's handshake policy. Maybe he came up with it on his own. Maybe I just never noticed and actually have an extra hand-caressin' handshake. Whatever. My handshake clearly threatened this 'lo's masculinity, which brings up a topic that deserves a look: does the Juggalo Family accept the LGBTQ community? ICP do their usual ambivalent moral flip-flopping when it comes to queer acceptance. But how do Juggalos on a ground level accept LGBTQ people into the fold? As a subculture claiming to accept outsiders and not tolerate bigots, noting where they stand on this is crucial.

Violent J claims to have no problems with gay people, but also seems to have no problem whatsoever throwing around the word faggot. And ICP often regulates on haters and rivals by associating them with dick-sucking. Overall, ICP seems genuinely intimidated by any threat to the hyper-masculine hegemony, and it extends far beyond handshakes. But what about the Juggalo Family? I certainly heard plenty of Juggalos call each other 'faggot' at The Gathering, but that merely shows their ignorance, and since ICP encourages ignorance, this is expected. Especially when I consider how common homophobia is in the impoverished communities where a lot of the Juggalos live. Not to mention the fact that Juggalos originated in the inherently backward and homophobic American culture. So for the sake of story, I'll give the Juggalos a mulligan on their on-the-surface-slurring and dig a little deeper to see how they might really feel about the LGBTQ community.

To deny the misogyny and homophobia of the larger hip hop culture (and by proxy, its influence on ICP and Wicked Shit) would be hypocritical. Homophobia is woven into the very fiber of hip hop. I tolerate bigoted, homophobic lyrics in rap more than other styles of music, not because I excuse it, but because it's so ubiquitous to the genre. You put up with it so you can continue listening. Much of hip hop historically relies, rather weak-mindedly, on the gender binary and regressive hyper-masculine tendencies. I could cite many reasons for this, from the fact that rap rose from the streets, where an outward display of "strength" coincides with survival, to the possibly that rappers, DJs, and graffiti writers battle for dominance in a competition-oriented subculture. Whatever the reason, a progressive hip hop fan finds a way to justify a culture, digressing to the point where many

MC battles are merely two rappers finding fresh ways to accuse each other of being gay for three rounds.

When I bring up this point, fans often counter with arguments like "that's not all hip hop" or "that's just gangsta rap" or "that's just mainstream rap." Sure, record labels throw money at rappers who shock and stir-up controversy because they sell more albums, but blaming misogyny and homophobia on a particular style of rap that isn't your cup of tea is a copout. And while plenty of hip hop artists aren't intolerant in this way, one questions the prevalence of it, and the fact that fans tolerate this bigotry. When an MC disses another by calling them "faggot" to imply weakness, or throws out the "no homo" phrase after rapping about other MCs being on their dicks, they create a breeding ground for bigotry and close-mindedness within the culture, while further alienating and marginalizing minorities. These acts constantly reaffirm straight male hegemony. Even some "conscious" rappers fall into this, and liberal and progressive rap fans excuse the behavior (take, for instance, Mos Def, who dissed other rappers by saying, "cats who claimin' they hard be mad fag/ so I run through 'em like flood water through sandbags"). The progressive rap fan might make compromises out of jadedness to the bigoted language's ubiquity, or maybe they don't want to dismiss some of the more positive messages a rapper says. Either way, this tolerance comes from a lack of shock at the genre's understated fear and hatred of LGBTQ people, and subjugation of anything associated with the feminine. This sets a precedent that has festered in rap to the point where unapologetic bigots can violently target LGBTQ folks with little reprisal. Such as the well-respected MC of Jedi Mind Tricks, Vinnie Paz, who spits vile lyrics like "listen I ain't gonna play no more, beat a faggot 'til he ain't fucking gay no more," which no longer just degrades, but actually targets gay people.

Fortunately, more and more music journalists, bloggers, and rappers themselves (like Kanye West and Snoop Dogg, who both came out in defense of the LGBT community), address and deconstruct these important topics. What's important here is seeing how the bigotry and misogyny of hip hop culture has influenced the Juggalo Family. Since Wicked Shit exists as an offshoot of rap, the music echoes some of the larger hip hop community's knuckle-dragging vernacular. But how does it translate to the Juggalo Family, a group that claims to accept outsiders?

My pre-Gathering research revealed little. Looking up "gay + Juggalo" only revealed Juggalos and non-Juggalos insulting each other on internet forums. Save for a few bisexual male Juggalos on Juggalo dating sites (yes, they have them), I found little. The existence of J-FLAG (Juggalo Family of Lesbians and Gays) impressed me, but they appear inactive. It seemed The Gathering was the only place I'd get the scoop.

"No, I don't have a problem with gay people," Kentucky enthusiastically tells me. "If that's what you're into, then that's fine."

Most Juggalos I talk to share the same attitude when asked, but that only includes Juggalos I'm able talk to. I don't talk to Juggalos who throw trash all day and chant for titties. But then again, a lot of those Juggalos are close to high school age. My friends and I were also loose with those words in high school, and if what I hear on the street is any indication, most teenage boys still call each other faggots. My short conversations with Juggalos of the more close-minded sort end poorly, often with me moving along out of fear of catching a beatdown (for not being a Juggalo), or them moving along out of fear of a fey handshake.

"If you're Fam, you're Fam," Juggalos who allow me to broach the topic repeatedly answer. Nonetheless, I get the impression they spend little time thinking about it at all, as if they've never really had to face it. That said, they really aren't losing any sleep over it, either. It's none of their business. In this way, the Juggalo Family transcends the less-than-progressive backgrounds most of them come from. Despite the numerous Wicked Shit songs referring to butt-fucking and dick-sucking as weak acts, when it comes to tribalism and community, many Juggalos care for their own enough to show respect.

I can't deny the obvious, though; there really aren't a lot of queer folks out here. Sid, the one openly queer person I meet, views his treatment in the Family positively. He's a trans man who totally gets down with the Clown.

"I feel accepted here, 'cause it's really not no big thing," Sid says. He identifies in the Family as lesbian. but not always as transgender.

"As a trans person, though... 'Cause I am trans, as well. Female to male. I don't know. I don't really tell too many people that shit. Normally, I'll just tell people that I prefer male pronouns or to just call me by my name and that's usually what they do. I've had, like, a couple homies back where I live who are like, 'you have tits, you're a chick,' and that's fucked up, but it's because of how you were taught and whatever, how you were raised. It's got nothing to do with being a Juggalo, like they still accept me as Family and shit. But, you know, they step on my toes with that shit, but whatever. And here, ya know, the only thing that really pisses me off is just hearing 'fag' all the time but that's everywhere. And it's just like, it sucks, but whatever. I've heard about two gay Juggalos holding hands by the lake. So, it's here."

Sid also retells a rumor he heard about Shaggy and Violent J intervening to break up a gay-bashing at one of their shows. When he brings up this evidence, I assume he's thought about it quite a bit. Like he tries to find stuff to help alleviate his alienation from not having fellow queer folks in the Juggalo Family. But he still feels comfortable and accepted, at least enough to stick around. He loves the Fam because he "came out with only ten bucks in his pocket," but the Juggalos took care of him, giving him all the food and weed he couldn't afford. As he talks to me about his experiences in the Family as trans, his Juggalo friends nod approval and back him up.

"Yeah… I don't feel like, 'hell, yeah! I can come out here with my packet and shit and, like, be a big trans dyke and shit,' 'cause people will probably be like 'uhh… what the fuck?' I'm not a big fan of that, but I also feel like if I were to do that they wouldn't care too much, either. It's just be, like, to each his own. Shit, it's not shit, you know, like you wanna be a trans dyke or whatever, do your thing," Sid says.

"Yeah, just do your thing. That's a perfect way to put it," Topher agrees.

I never get to the bottom of it out here, since I simply cannot talk to every Juggalo at the Gathering, nor do I sit down and deconstruct the lyrics to homophobic ICP songs with Juggalos. I don't get the chance ask every Juggalo why they flippantly toss around faggot as an insult. I certainly am not able to get into in any complex discussions of sexuality. Also, most of the Juggalos I meet try to prove to me the open-minded awesomeness of their Family, which skews the information I collect. Simply speaking to the Juggalos who willingly talk to me, however faulty a control group, many express the same sentiment as Sid and Topher: just do your thing.

# TWIZTID SEMINAR

*No more knocking on the door,*

*We moshing on the floor and shit,*

*And we ain't leaving till we heaving up some blood and shit,*

*Fuck a mothafucking Twix, bitch,*

*I'd rather roll with the clique of lunatics,*

*That's now known as TWIZTID!!*

– Monoxide Child of Twiztid, "Juggalo Party"

A few thousand bodies once again cram into the stifling heat of the Seminar Tent, this time for the Twiztid seminar. Loud shop fans blow from the stage onto the crowd, but offer little relief. The heat is so sweltering that most of the 'los give up on the face paint. One Juggalo, a thin guy in his early twenties with short cropped hair, holds tight, sweating through his make-up. Beads of sweat cascade down the pasty white and glaring green of his clown face, but his hand resists reaching to wipe it. He just stares at the empty stage intently. He wears the more gothic Juggalo look, less common than the baggy streetwear style—tight, black pants tucked into tall platform boots with lots of straps stopping just above the knee. I'm nauseated and groggy from the heat, but still feel a twinge of pity for how much more uncomfortable he must be. I see him around the Gathering frequently and, though I haven't approached him, everything about him screams true believer.

A huge "*Whoop! Whoop!*" rises up from the crowd as Twiztid struts onto the stage. They wear matching oversized t-shirts with red and black gothic lettering and a picture of an eagle with spread wings. Monoxide Child (born Paul Methric), the skinnier one, wears a red ball cap backward and tilted to the side. Jamie Madrox (born Jamie Spaniolo), the self-proclaimed fat one, wears three small braids on the top of his head in a line. Neither are wearing makeup. I can't tell from where I stand if they're wearing their trademark evil contacts.

"What up, y'all?" Monoxide addresses the crowd. "It's a lot cooler in here," he says referring to the fans blowing behind them onstage,

"How are ya?"

The Juggalos answer back in a torrent of shouting and *Whoop! Whoop!*ing

"Did someone get stabbed? Was I misinformed?" Monoxide asks the crowd with a smile.

Another huge "*Whoop! Whoop!*" comes up from the crowd. Aside from the Tila attack, the only other notable assault at The

Gathering was between two carnies fighting over backstage passes, which ended in a stabbing, or so the rumor goes. After addressing the stabbing, Madrox and Monoxide start riffing, beginning with the weather. Madrox, the fat one, proposes a winter gathering, and the audience yells a huge "*Whoop! Whoop!*"

"I'll have, you know, I'm gonna start pre-selling tickets to my winter gathering," he says in a ragged and croaking voice, and gets the 'los *Whoop! Whoop!*ing again.

"As it sits, I have six tickets sold," he continues, "So that means there's six fat kids here that would love to have Faygo snowball Armageddon…"

"*Whoop! Whoop!*"

"The Snow Boot Running Challenge…"

"*Whoop! Whoop!*"

"The Who-Put-The-Dick-On-The-Snowman Challenge…"

"*Whoop! Whoop!*"

"Here's what I see," Monoxide chimes in, "me onstage… urine-soaked snowballs…" he says, feigning lobbing one into the air. Then he shouts, "I'm gonna poop in this one," and pantomimes another throw.

The Juggalos laugh loudly.

"If one of y'all threw a diarrhea ball at me, we wouldn't be friends no more. I'd just have to cut the relationship off. But, man, if I got hit with feces, I thought it was all love."

The Juggalos laugh more.

"This year the love was strong. I got hit with one of everything in this bitch. Beer cans. Bottles of pop. Someone threw an RV sink at me. What up, fam?" Monoxide calls out.

"I want to know who the Keystone Bandit is, the guy who's got the shittiest beer in the world. They like grip 'em like fucking grenades," he says, imitating pulling out the pin on an imaginary can of Keystone. "And they scope people. This guy has accuracy. No matter where you are he will scope you out and get your motherfuckin' ass."

The Juggalos just keep cracking up and *Whoop! Whoop!*ing.

They segue back into Madrox joking about the heat, about how he "saw ninjas on the side of the road with heatstroke and people looking all lifeless and dead like an Alice In Chains song."

"We spent two whole nights riding around the campground just to make sure that people weren't dead," Monoxide says.

"Passing out little Dixie cups of water," Madrox continues.

"Giving them a little pat on the balls," adds Monoxide.

The Juggalos laugh hysterically.

"Here drink this Dixie Cup. Stay hydrated. Like, I could piss more than a Dixie Cup," pronounces Madrox.

"That'll be three dollars," says Monoxide.

"Right. How are you gonna charge three dollars for a Dixie Cup of water?" Madrox asks.

"A motherfucker tried to sell me a sandwich bag full of dirt and grass, saying, 'I got Gathering crops for four bucks!'" Monoxide claims.

"Oh, c'mon, it's like pieces of the Berlin Wall. This is official Lake Hepatitis water and you know how it's official 'cause of the rubber band on the top and not like the rubber band you put around your money, it's the cock rubber band from the rubber,'" exclaims Madrox, making a toss-off motion in front of his crotch. "That's how you know it's official, and I know some of y'all still got your towels still on. I'm a let you know, we done told you y'all every year: Lake Hepatitis is a no-go for the Juggalo," he continues amid more laughter from the Juggalos.

"But I can't front, for some of them motherfuckers—it's either Lake Hepatitis or die," Monoxide says, throwing a bone to the audience, because after all, the lake offers the only escape from the heat.

"Fair enough," Madrox banters back. "But, okay, here's the condom and you're swimming," he flails his arms imitating a Juggalo frog-stroking the condom away from him, "trying to get away from it and it's got a little milk in it. I know that ain't frosting because I ain't had no Pop Tart."

The Juggalos convulse and reel with laughter, shaking and folding over in the heat. It almost seems rehearsed—the way Jamie and Madrox volley off each other. One bounces around behind the other with sound effects, acting out what the other describes. Moving from one topic to the next, sometimes rehashing a previous crowd favorite (like the Lake Hepatitis condom), and the Family roars with approval. They act like of a bunch of high school or college friends sitting around a particle board coffee table, bloated with beer spillage, passing a bong in their first apartment, trying to outdo each other in gross-out jokes. But Twiztid ties the crowd around their finger.

Madrox excitedly retells a story about when they found Star Trek cereal at a store in a town near here.

"We were all hype. We had our milk. We sat down with our bowls. We looked at the expiration date and that bitch was from two years ago."

"Stardate, 1987, captain's log," Monoxide dramatically announces.

"We ate the shit. It was super nasty, but we ate the shit. We were going to bring the rest out and throw it out like duck feed and just see who wanted to catch it. Mite, mite, mite," Madrox imitates a duck quacking. "Sprinklin' y'all with marshmallows and lil Cinnabons 'n' shit."

This leads to a debate over Star Trek versus Star Wars. They consider themselves fans of both, but Monoxide prefers Star Wars and Madrox prefers Star Trek. Madrox's choice elicits some boos from the Juggalos.

"When it goes down," says Madrox, dissing Luke Skywalker, "he's riding in a broke down Landspeeder with two droids and Captain Kirk's up there fucking some green bitch, like, yeah."

He goes on saying Captain Kirk taught him everything he knows about sex.

"I'm like, let me beam you up! Let me beam you up," he says thrusting his crotch, while Monoxide mimics the theme song into the microphone.

After some time, someone in their crew finds the Star Trek cereal and passes it to the stage. Madrox gets his wish and walks across the front of the stage, emptying the box into the open hands and mouths of the Juggalos.

"Mite, mite, mite," he says.

They start taking questions from the audience. A Juggalette gets up and asks if she can get her bong signed and a hug from Madrox. They agree to sign the bong, but not to the hug. Most of the Juggalos asking for autographs claim they stood in line for hours but the autograph session still ended before they could get theirs. They sign a few, but then cut it off. Otherwise, that's all they'd do.

"You better not ask for an autograph," he says to a 'lette in the crowd, but it's not an autograph she wants.

"Can I have a hug from you guys?" she asks.

They turn her down, but other 'lettes keep trying. The Juggalettes flirt with Twiztid, the sex stars of the Psychopathic Family, especially the hefty Madrox, an unconventional heartthrob. The Juggalettes seem to flock to them because of their psychosexual lyrics.

"Heyyy, Jamie and Paul," a young, thin 'lette says addressing them in an overly sensual, flirty falsetto.

"Heyyy," they tease her in unison.

"I was wondering. I know you all rhyme about some crazy sexual shit you do. Well, what's the craziest freakiest sexual shit you've ever done?"

"You got about two hours, I'll tell you some shit," Monoxide says.

"That's like some personal intimate shit and if we tell it and we get intimate with some bitch, she'll be like all he did was just have sex with me. He didn't piss in my ear like he said he would onstage. He didn't rub his ass cheek on my titty. You're gonna steal all my Jedi Secrets, I can't tell those."

When a Juggalo brings up Tila Tequila, Monoxide says, "We ain't going to talk about that, because we all see it a different way. There's no sense in creating a line."

A Juggalo from the crowd with a stoned-sounding voice says he bought a jersey that his friend told him was one of only two made. He asks Twiztid to verify the legitimacy of the statement.

"Oh, for real," Madrox says. "You want that approved. No, there was more than two of those made. They lied to you." But then tells him it's still dope and not a bootleg.

I don't know why, but I keep hoping for a 'lo to question why they only played half a set. Part of me wants to think at least one Juggalo felt he got a raw deal after coming this far.

One Juggalo gets up and says,

"After your abbreviated set last night, I heard a couple people talking some shit on the new album and I want to say, 'fuck that.' That shit was hot. I loved it."

They thank him and say the Juggalos can think whatever they want, but Twiztid still put together the album for them. They made it as gift and aren't mad if the 'los don't like it.

"Last year, didn't you say that you were going to bring something special to the Gathering?" a Juggalo asks.

"We did, it was a record. It's the most special thing we could think of next to our children. Right now that's the thing that means the absolute most to us. and to share it with y'all, it was the shit," Monoxide responds.

The next girl in line says she intended to ask her question to ICP, but the seminar ended before she got a chance. It's about the importance of the Number 17, a number crucial to ICP mythology, and a sort of legendary nod to the mere seventeen copies sold on the release day of ICP's first album. The number also has a lot of synchronicity with Violent J and Shaggy, which they apply to the Dark Carnival. The question is long, meandering and hard to follow, so Monoxide cuts her off,

"Do your research on ICP and the Number 17. It will explain it all. Thank you for coming. Sit back down."

"It looks like her first gathering, we were all Gathering virgins at one time," Madrox says playfully to the rest of the Family. "I'm just saying, for everyone who's ready to Tila Tequila." His tone gets real.

"Let me explain something to you. This is what I've learned," Monoxide says. "There's two sets of Juggalos. There's the motherfuckers who wear the paint all the time and just live the shit, right? I mean fuckin' live it"

The platform-booted Juggalo nods somberly through his green painted on grin. Monoxide goes on, "And then there's the other who just… casually… They like it. They dig the music, they dig the atmosphere. They don't necessarily paint up but they'll come out to the shows, buy your merch or whatever. The crazy thing is y'all can't get along. What I don't understand is where the separation came between y'all; that shit is insane to me. I don't know where the message got twisted. It's a whole other seminar, but it's something to think about. I want to know what makes these Juggalos so much better than these Juggalos. I want to hear it for real, 'cause I'm baffled by the shit."

The Juggalos grow quiet and listen intently for a moment, leaving out the cheering and *Whoop! Whoop!*ing.

"If it's real Family Love, then look out for your motherfuckin' Family. Or we need to make up a new word and quit frontin'," he continues.

"*Distant cousin! Distant cousin!*" Madrox chants into the mic.

" 'Cause that's what it's like. You see a motherfucker layin', pukin' in the shit and everybody like 'let's go kick 'em'. If that's your Family help that motherfucker out. Set him up. Get him an ice-cold water. Show the Love."

"I'll tell you a hundred percent, a Juggalo is a Juggalo," Madrox says. "To bomb on somebody because they're not as hardcore as you is wack."

"That's why we come out with no paint on, so the shock will wear off. So y'all will understand," Monoxide explains.

The Juggalos quietly listen, mesmerized.

"We're just like you. There's nothing different between me and you but the microphone, and we speak for you, so you should respect that,' Madrox declares. 'If you want to leave here and kick a Juggalo and then go home and think about it, that's fine. I'm not tellin' ya what to do. I'm not your daddy. I'm your brother. And if we love each other we can grow as a family and not as a cult. Not as a bunch of mindless fuckers who don't know. Respect the motherfucker next to you. Respect the bitch next to you."

The Juggalos *"Whoop! Whoop!"* Loudly in agreement. Then time runs out. The seminar ends.

# BREAKING DOWN CAMP

*Ain't nobody jealous, everybody has they own*
*Nobody locked up, everybody, everybody is free to roam*
*Lookin' at scrubby with a hottie on his side*
*Lookin' at rich kids, poor kids,*
*Everybody together on the same side*
*And they down to ride*

*Let's go all the way*
*(Let's go all the way)*
*Let's go all the way*
*Let's go all the way*

*Ain't nobody left out, everybody gets to go*
*It can never be too crowded, come on, we still pickin' up*
*some more*
*Don't nobody hate you, playa hate you,*

*There ain't no hate at all*
*Gotta million hands to catch you cause they'll catch you*
*And they never will let you fall*
*And we gotta worry all of y'all*

*Let's go all the way*
*(Let's go all the way)*
*Let's go all the way*
*Let's go all the way*

*Never known sickness, no sickness, nobody has to die*
*Everything's answered, what didn't then, we'll never have to*
*wonder why*
*Won't nobody rush you, no pressure, be as long as you*
*wanna be*
*Can't you guess what this place is,*
*Your future make it a reality*
*all you have to do is follow me*

*Let's go all the way*
*(Let's go all the way)*
*Let's go all the way*
*Let's go all the way*

– Insane Clown Posse, "Let's Go All the Way"

"I let you guys run shit for a while. Now I gotta get mine," says a Black guy in a Chicago Bulls basketball jersey to a small, dirty, long-haired white kid .

The kid holds a sign written on 12-pack cardboard saying, "Rolls ~~$15.00~~ ~~$10.00~~ ~~$7.00~~ $5.00." In Chicago's outward palm lays a packet of colorful blue pills, presumably of a higher quality.

"I'm just trying to get home," the kid says.

So much trash litters the ground, at this point it equals the amount of visible earth. We just kick through it as we walk and duck when it flies. The Juggalos are stoked because ICP takes the stage in a few hours. Still, a melancholy permeates the air as everyone breaks down their camps, packing up the physical manifestation of the Dark Carnival, leaving their hearts to carry it on until the next Gathering.

Everyone spent all their money, and are left hustling anything and everything for gas. A few drugs remain for sale on Drug Bridge, but they've mostly been replaced with a lot more of everything else. You can get as many Jell-O shots as you can carry for $5 bucks. Packs of cigarettes get dumped into piles, sold for fifty cents apiece. Swigs of whiskey or vodka go for whatever one can throw down. Apparently titty-flashes still work as currency, and near me a couple smoke bombs go off.

"Hey ninja, are you writing?" A Juggalo asks me on Drug Bridge, breaking me out of the spell of writing all of this down in my small black journal.

"Oh… yeah… " I say.

"I was just asking because I've never seen anybody writing here before. What are you writing about?"

"Oh, just all of this, you know, what I'm experiencing."

"That's cool," he says.

I pull out my camera to take a few pictures.

"Hey, what kind of camera is that?" a big Juggalo asks me as he walks by with a group of four other pretty big dudes.

"Um, a Nikon," I stammer, not sure what to say.

"'A Nikon,' his buddy mocks. 'It's a Nikon,'" his tone vaguely threatening.

I'm not sure where this is going, but I'm starting to wonder if I wore out my welcome. I wonder if I said too much about my purpose when blacked out at some point. I put my camera back in my bag and head back to the van.

•       •       •

The clouds move in as Damon and I sit in the van with the side door open, taking turns on our last fifth of whiskey. The impending rain thickens the air and is a welcome respite from the demoralizing heat. We hand our fifth off to whoever moseys by the van. Some we know well by now, while others we just meet. It reminds me of the old days: Damon and I, somewhere we don't belong, acting like a couple of dumbasses and laughing a lot, nearing the end of our adventure.

"Aw, man, it looks like it's that time," I tell Damon, and get up to take a shit.

We both avoided the mortifying porta-potties, prolonging the inevitable by packing ourselves with nothing but summer sausage and cheese.

"Get a clean break," he advises.

I refuse to use the porta-potties, choosing to shit in the woods instead. I grab a roll of toilet paper and head off the property, under a barbed wire fence, past a cop parked off property in an Explorer guarding the road. I turn to head down into a ravine when I find a carpet of poison ivy. I think back to the porta-potties, cross my fingers, hoping I still possess the immunity I had as a kid, and plow right through it down the ravine. I find a dry gully, squat down and do my business.

As I scramble through the brush to get out, the sprinkling starts. Soon comes the heavy, cold, Midwestern rain of my youth. The sky dumps the redemptive torrents I left behind long ago for Seattle's steady drizzle. The rain soaks my clothes, mud clings to the fabric as I scramble out of the ravine, and I shiver and smile. I'm far away from all the trash and merchandise, and aside for a few RVs and trailers, I'm isolated. I walk back, drunk on whiskey, and gaze up through my spotted glasses into the pouring shower. The thick film of Hepatitis Lake washes away, along with my own sweat and the grime of Hogrock. I head back to the van and sit on the bumper, getting soaked in the downpour.

The shower ends and kicks a glorious lavender sunset across the sky.

"Check that out," I say to a Juggalette parked near us. "Fucking amazing."

"What... ?" She asks, and then sees me pointing.

"The sunset," I say.

"Oh... yeah... " she says.

I notice she's changing in between two cars into an outfit to wear to ICP's show tonight. I realize she might think I'm referring to her half-dressed state, thinking she was being leered at yet again. But maybe the sunset just doesn't impress her. I continue to watch the sun go down, cooled off and renewed. Living in Seattle with its misty drizzle, I often miss the heavy rain and thunderstorms of the Midwest and the South, the comforting ambiance of a downpour and the funny feeling I get in my stomach and spine when I hear thunder crack and roll. Nature's spell is soon broken by a couple of cars pulling away from the campsite.

"What the fuck?" A Juggalo in full face-paint exclaims, throwing his arms up in confused frustration." They're leaving before ICP! Why the fuck would you do that, 'lo? That's fucked up."

"I don't know, ninja," I say and shrug, a bit jarred.

"Hey, has Spice 1 played yet?" I ask him, remembering where I am.

It turns out Spice 1, an old school gangsta rap MC, canceled, along with Slick Rick, so I miss another act I hoped to see. ICP often relays how hard it is to get acts to play the Gathering, and how a lot of them back out at the last minute (particularly ones I want to see). Damon wakes up, comes up over my shoulder, and hands me the whiskey bottle.

"Time to live the chaos," he says, grinning.

I wash down the last of the Vicodin we scored the night before, and we head to the main stage.

We run into Nathan and Samantha on the way. A white garbage bag filled with beer hangs over Nathan's shoulder and a thick layer of white greasepaint covers his face. Samantha dresses the same.

"Hey. How's it goin'?" I ask. "You look prepared."

"Hey, what's up?" Nathan says, his features still readable beneath the paint. "Man, I'm stoked to see ICP! I know the Juggalos can be a bit ridiculous, but ICP is still the best live band that I've ever seen."

He still wears his fitted indie-rocker-looking t-shirt, but blends in just the same. We follow them towards the stage, lose them in the crowd, and wait for Method Man and Redman.

"What up, Illinois?" Meth shouts to the crowd between songs.

Damon and I give each other a look that reads, "Shit, no one here is from Illinois."

The forgiving audience shouts out, "*Whoop! Whoop!*"

I'm super stoked to see Method Man, to the point I'd see the show anywhere. Method Man may not be considered the best rapper in Wu-Tang Clan, but he was always my favorite. I appreciate the apocalyptic nature of his solo albums and his overall aesthetic.

"How many of y'all smokin' some shit, tonight?" Meth shouts to the crowd, who return with a "*Whoop! Whoop!*"

They then go into a familiar Wu-Tang hit.

"Hey you, get off my cloud, you don't know me and you don't know my style."

And another "*Whoop! Whoop!*" rises from the crowd. Wicked Shit or not, most of the Juggalos know the song.

"I got fat bags of sku-unk, I got White Owl blu-unts… " Meth and Redman throw out the call, holding the mic out to the audience.

"And I'm about to go get lifted… about to go get lifted," the 'los and I shout back.

"I've got myself a forty and I've got myself a shorty and…"

"I'm about to go and stick it… about to go and stick it."

A few bottles fly at the stage, streaks of water flash in the stage lights. The song ends to a cheer and even more, "*Whoop! Whoop!*"s.

"What up, Illinois?" Redman says again, throwing his arm back and forth rhythmically.

The Juggalos start chanting "*Fam-uh-lee! Fam-uh-lee!*" as Meth and Redman go into the next song.

"That bottle almost hit me, yo. Don't be throwin' shit," Meth shouts to the audience.

Next song. More stuff is tossed at the stage, but most of the Juggalos just have a great time shouting the choruses and throwing their arms in the air.

"*Fam-uh-lee! Fam-uh-lee!*" go the Juggalos.

Communication breaks down between Meth and Redman and the Juggalos. Meth seems obtuse to his audience or location. Redman speaks into his ear between songs, explaining something we can't hear. They move into another song. At the end of it the crowd cheers and then,

"*Fam-uh-lee! Fam-uh-lee!*"

"What?" Meth asks the crowd.

"*Fam-uh-lee! Fam-uh-lee!*"

Redman walks over to him and says something. I notice a few middle fingers fly up from the crowd, but most of the 'los are still getting down.

"*Fam-uh-lee! Fam-uh-lee!*"

"What?" Meth asks again.

"*Fam-uh-lee! Fam-uh-lee!*"

"What? Family? Fuck family! This is about hip hop!"

A split forms between the crowd. Some of the 'los continue to get into the show, but more and more middle fingers rise up, and all the Juggalos unite in the chant "*Fam-uh-lee!*" as Meth and Redman go into their next song. Trash flies toward the stage as the DJ cuts the record short.

"Man, that shit almost hit me, that's fucked up stop throwing shit and we'll go on with the show."

*Fam-uh-lee! Fam-uh-lee! Fam-uh-lee!*

Then, in the middle of a song, a full glass bottle flies from the crowd and hits Meth in the face. Foam flies out everywhere as it hits him. He throws down the mic angrily.

"*Fuck the nigga who threw that!*" shouts Meth.

"*Fuck that shit! Fuck that shit! Fuck that shit!*" chants the majority of the Juggalos, pissed off at whoever threw it.

"Yo, your face is cut,' Redman says. 'You need to get that looked at."

"*Fuck that! I don't need this shit, man!*" he says. "*My heart don't bleed Kool-Aid!*"

"You need to get that shit checked out," Redman repeats.

*"Fuck that! Start the music! We're finishing the show!"* Meth says.

The DJ spins the record and starts the next song.

Blood pours down Meth's face as he wipes it off with a towel. They finish their set to a loud chanting of *"Fam-uh-lee!"* Throughout the crowd, middle fingers.

*"Fuck y'all, I don't bleed Kool-Aid!"* he repeats after the last song, and they walk off the stage, ending the most genuinely badass performance I've ever seen.

I heard rumors some 'los had it out for Method Man before he even said "Fuck Family," because of his mainstream success. I'm shocked that Method Man and Redman made it all the way here without having a clue where they were or who their audience was. Didn't their P.R. or management fill them in on the Juggalos? Did they assume the Gathering was a music festival like any other? Who knows. Maybe they smoked too much before the show. Meth's Wu-Tang Clan is one of the most classic and well-respected hip hop crews. They're famous because they changed the game, not because they played pop, and they're some of the hardest and dopest rappers ever. They're O.G. I can't imagine why anybody would fuck with them.

Next up: ICP.

•          •          •

*"Fam-uh-lee! Fam-uh-lee! Fam-uh-lee! Fam-uh-lee! Fam-uh-lee! Fam-uh-lee!"*

The Juggalos chant to a dark stage before ICP's set. I take a swill off my whiskey, the Vicodin warm and fuzzy in my stomach. Then… *Bang! Pow! Boom!* and a fifty-foot set of lights washes over the crowd. A blinking Hatchetman lights up on stage, followed by a blazing I, followed by a C, and then a P.

Finally, "ICP" comes on pulsing and blinding in its glory. The Hatchetman right beside it, blinking on and off.

*"Do you know who you're fucking with?"* A looped sample pounds the audience, and a heavy metal guitar riff backs the shouted, *"W-w-w-w-w-w-w-Wicked! Wicked clown!"* followed by a sampled gun blast. *"Ka-pow!"*

Violent J and Shaggy hit the stage all painted up and chuck two-liters of Faygo into the crowd. The crowd responds with a thundering, *"Whoop! Whoop!"* A warm chill runs up my spine.

"My father was a priest cold-blooded he's dead, Hypocrite, he was a bigot so I cut off his head, poured out the holy water 'bless the dead' is what I said, and heard the demons screamin' as his body bled," Insane Clown Posse raps.

*"W-w-w-w-w-w-w-Wicked clown! W-w-w-w-w-w-w-Wicked clown! Don't fuck with me!"*

"… Hey babe, why don't ya chill and kill this two-liter, went into my trailer, I filled up the glass, before she took a sip I had my dick in her ass… " goes the rhyme.

Clowns, monsters, demons, dance around Violent J and Shaggy, soaking the Family down with Faygo. The bass throbs, looped by a DJ spinning records behind a protective clear plastic sneeze guard. He throws his hands in the air, bouncing between the two turntables. I put my camera away to protect it and taste the salty, sugary, citrus liquid running down my face as a big, fat clown with a rainbow wig and a puffy red nose wets down the 'los with a fire hose of Red Mist. Violent J and Shaggy go into number after number.

"If I only could, I'd set the world on fire. Say *'Fuck the world! Fuck the world!'*"

*"Fuck the world! Fuck the world!"* the crowd shouts back.

Shaggy and Violent J clutch their cordless mics in one hand and rap, while shaking up 2-liter bottles of Faygo in the other; they loosen the caps and douse the open-mouthed Juggalos. Titties get soaked as Juggalettes gleefully writhe in the spray. Violent J starts drop-kicking bottle after bottle of the sticky generic soda into the crowd. Grinning rubber-masked clowns in baggy red and yellow jumpsuits refresh the supply with crate after crate of Faygo.

*"Fuck the world! Fuck the world!"* ICP and the Juggalos chant.

Bottles fly through the air non-stop, and the Juggalos lose their fucking minds. They hug and pass blunts while shouting out the choruses. Beach balls bounce all throughout the crowd, tight fists pound them away from wherever they land. On both sides of me, Juggalo couples embrace, kissing deeply in the cloying mist. This is it! The moment they live for! The crowd pulsates with life, moving in waves as one giant unit. Someone passes me a joint. I hit it. *Whoop! Whoop!* Everybody is rolling on E, tripping on acid or mushrooms, blunted as fuck or in a drunken stupor. The thick air sparks with unity.

"*Fam-uh-lee! Fam-uh-lee! Fam-uh-lee!*" The crowd chants as a song fades… "*Fam-uh-lee! Fam-uh-lee!*" When these chants quiet an electric hush fills the air, punctured by a few scattered "*Whoop! Whoop!*"s. And I get another chill…

I hear a tinkling piano, the beginning of a song I know. ICP begins their power ballad, "If I Was a Serial Killer." Violent J's voice breaks in, poignantly singing.

"If I was a serial killer, they'd find all my victims' heads in funky ass gas station toilets." The crowd sings along, "And if I was a serial killer, I would be strange and deranged. And I would never change."

The emotion of the crowd crackles, understated by the calm tension of the ballad. Some lighters go up in the air. The Faygo slows to a pour from the shaken-up propulsion of the faster, heavier songs.

"If I was a Serial Killer, I'd be known as The Smoker, 'cause I'd cut off and smoke all they hair and if I was a Serial Killer I would sleep on broken glass and thumbtacks and I would smoke mad crack," ICP and the Family sings. It's a perverted, yet tender moment.

Hands and lighters wave back and forth in the air. The stage goes dark for a minute as a piano loop plays out the end of the song.

Then a heavy beat kicks off and the giant, blinking I… C… P lights once again flood the audience with dizzying light.

"*Whoop! Whoop!*" Go the Juggalos.

The Hatchetman comes back on, pulsing and pounding. The evil clowns and demons come dancing back out, along with a few elite chubby 'los and 'lettes slipping and sliding on the stage, spraying more Faygo on the audience.

My head struggles to make sense of everything. My body is full of the warm, buzzy, twist of whiskey, Vicodin, and Clown Love—but something pushes its way to the front of my mind, fighting its way through the oneness of the crowd. I try to catch hold of it, but I lose it. I think about all the songs that filled my ears this evening, remembering all of them from my years of worthless scrutiny, and how goddamned stupid I found them before. The Faygo soda combines with the dust in the air and a thick, grimy film covers my body; it may be disgusting, but this is the best show I've ever seen. It embodies the Dark Carnival—it's rapturous, godlike, and as near holy as anything I saw or felt in the Pentecostal church growing up. It reminds me of God's flock thrashing about the church, shouting out in tongues and falling straight to the floor, slain in the spirit after the pastor firmly pressed his palm to their forehead. I bat a beach ball away from me. Generous, offering hands hold more joints out to me. I take long drags off them. I pass my whiskey around, and the Juggalos take it, grins plastered on their faces, their eyes turning back to the stage as they swig from the bottle.

I move to a safer distance, out of the spray, to take it all in. This is what it's all about, I think. Pure carbonated shock and awe. Faygo soaks the crowd and they work themselves into a frenzy of devotion and Wicked Clown Love. Nothing but Clown Love. At least thirty people bounce around the stage, still shaking and spraying and chucking two-liters of Faygo into the crowd. I lick the citrusy corn syrup from my upper lip. My hair is soaked and ratted, my hand catches when I push it from my face. It's impossible to deny the sheer power of this concert, of the clown faces of Violent J and Shaggy, the wicked mask continually worn representing all of the love and humanity the 'los might ever witness.

I wipe Rock & Rye Faygo from my eyes and stare deep into ICP's faces, eyes glassy and awash in Clown Love. ICP's sophomoric, scatological rhymes blend together. I realize I was off track looking for the answers in ICP lyrics to explain this culture. I move toward the stage as torrents of Faygo pour down on me, my gaze fixed on the faces of Insane Clown Posse. The Juggalos don't take notice of me or the spell that I'm under.

I stare into the clown masks. I get it now. This is why someone becomes a Juggalo. I take a slug on my bottle of whiskey and realize that, in this moment, I may be the only one of these 20,000 people not experiencing complete bliss. I fixate on Violent J's clown face as he moves about the stage and feel my shirt collar stick to my neck.

*"Whoop! Whoop!"* the crowd cries out.

I watch Shaggy's mouth move, but fail to hear the stage banter coming out of it. All of my obsessively trying to figure out this odd subculture boils down to this one loud and charismatic concert. Is this what makes a "Juggalo for life"? And these two clowns... I keep staring into their faces, and I suspect they'll begin to mock me with their leering painted-on smiles, but I only see two very lucky charismatic leaders. Prophets. Pimps. The Wicked Clown face hiding a couple of willfully ignorant, possibly psychopathic rappers from the slums of Detroit. Too hateful or fearful of knowledge to learn how magnets work, but with a single-minded expertise at sales and promotion, at processing their own greed. I see the Wicked Clown who came to Violent J in a dream to teach the path to Shangri-La.

As I soak in a communion of Faygo and the incense of grape blunts, I get hit with a full force blow of what's really going on and I no longer find it funny or compelling or fascinating. The narcotics in my system no longer fight my analytical mind and my irritation progresses. My skin becomes itchy, pores feel clogged with fructose, and I lose my ability to just go with the flow. My false euphoria wanes; I no longer feel the Juggalo Family's unity or even the warmth and rush of a great concert. The Family Love heartbeat throbs all around me but I stand still, staring into that clown face, forcing myself on this final night to process everything—and everything suddenly comes into focus.

The Wicked Clown. It's just one more fucking thing… one more thing for the poor and wretched of the earth to latch onto as an outlet for their rage at their poverty, their powerlessness. It acts as another distraction for the outcast, for the poor, for the downtrodden. I stare into the faces of the clowns on the stage. I look at J's grinning face. I don't see the benevolence that the Juggalos claim hides beneath the wicked facade. And I know underneath all the greasepaint, the clown laughs at the floobs and scrubs who follow them. Clown Love detaches from Insane Clown Posse as I stare into that grin. It was the Juggalos who made Clown Love what it is, and they did it themselves. They created a family to take care of each other, to defend each other. And I, this scrubby ex-punk rock kid trying to be a journalist, stare into the clown face and I see that it's not about the size of one's bank account, but the size of one's heart. And Juggalos got heart. They really got fucking heart. But I see no heart in the clown faces of Violent J and Shaggy; I just see greed and lust for power excused by the all too familiar tenets of prophecy and faith.

Faith. This former tongue-speaking Pentecostal kid sees it in the benediction on the stage. It's all too familiar. It ripples up my own spine, triggered by the crowd and fueled by Vicodin and booze. I recall my own mother feeling the wings of an angel caress her as she thrashed about the church, speaking in tongues when I was a child. My own father pounding the pulpit, screaming of damnation and the amens and weeping of the congregation as the organ played low. This is different, but still very familiar.

It also reminds me of more benevolent times—my first punk rock show, the pile-ons of kids shouting anthems into the mic, unknown hands picking me up when I fell in the mosh pit. How I, a scrawny, fucked up kid, walked out the doors of shows with the ammo to fight for everything I wanted.

I stare into the Clown Face and think of Twiztid telling the 'los how they speak for them, how they're equals. How graciously they gave away autographs and Star Trek Cereal. I think about the merch booth, and the Juggalos pressed against the chain link fence waiting for the doors to open. And all around me, fat girls become pretty and skinny boys become tough. Don't fuck with a Juggalo! This night exists for the floobs and the scrubs. Their night. Faygo pours into their wide-open mouths as the "*Whoop! Whoop!*"s grow louder and more and more earth-shaking. But I hear them as if underwater, multiple colors of Faygo drenching me. I continue to stare into the Clown Face as ICP goes into one of their old school numbers, "I Stuck Her with My Wang".

"I stuck her with my wang, she hit me in the balls, I grabbed her by her neck and I bounced her off the walls," goes the song. The Juggalos give up a final "*Whoop! Whoop!*"

I slip into a sort of hallucinatory state, hearing the Clown laugh in my head. I wonder how things would be if the Juggalos were given something beside Hatchet Gear and Psychopathic Records. I wonder what would happen if they broke free of the spell of Violent J and Shaggy 2 Dope and grabbed hold of their own power. Would they return to the Dark Carnival? Would they still be distracted by the prophecies, the wet t-shirt contests, and the Flashlight Wrestling? Would they plant a garden instead of eating elephant ears and drinking Faygo? Would they trade-in floob pride for a working class solidarity? Would they wave their hatchets at their oppressors? Would they get an education or simply educate themselves? Would Juggalettes find less joy in oil-wrestling and the bartering of titty flashes? I look at the Clown and the true shape of its wickedness stares back at me, laughing at me in my state of heightened awareness.

I look down, knowing I'll let down everyone here who trusted me, everyone who respected me, everyone I befriended by walking out of here and writing this down, talking shit about everything they love, everything they build their lives around. When it comes down to the wire—despite, or perhaps because of, the Clown Love I've felt—I'll walk out of Hogrock... and disrespect the Hatchet.

I grow tired, my arms heavy on my shoulders. I think of everyone I knew in the shitty old town of Milltown. I think of friends I left behind, never seeing them again. And how rumors catch up to me, rumors of meth-fueled heart attacks, infanticide, prison sentences for brutal murders. All this resides in the back of my mind, somewhere behind a sick, jaded, redneck joke and an elitist amnesia. I think of the dispossessed in that town who, indirectly, steered me toward all of this in the first place. The Clown's smile becomes a sneer. It mocks me because the Clown knows I'm onto him, but there's not a goddamn thing that I can do about it. The Clown sneer that blinds Violent J and Shaggy from their own detached selves as they search for the power taken from them as children, the false nobility of their prophecy, their vision, their Dark Carnival. The Wicked Clown represents a leadership leading its followers away from themselves, away from any true unified power. In this Clown's face—a pimp of poverty, fear, and traumas both mental and physical—I see an all-too-familiar-psychopathic lust for power and wealth. And the crowd, a shocking allegory for humanity itself, a cryptic reminder that we are all bleating sheep, a mass desperate for distraction from their struggles.

The Clown is the mocking face of power. We listen, we follow, and we don its wicked mask and become hoes to our own fear.

But the show goes on. I think of these Juggalos and their reverence to their mad and mentally-ill leaders, following a vague watered-down version of Judeo-Christian morality filtered through songs of misogyny and violence. I think of the Juggalos' kindness. Their love of their self-made family. Their community. I realize that the only good things the Juggalos have, are things they created themselves. They started the family. They take care of each other. They love each other. They always have each other's backs. A Juggalo never dies alone. They did this, not Violent J and Shaggy. Not the Dark Carnival, and not "God." A thunderous, final *"Whoop! Whoop!"* takes me out of my thoughts as the stage goes dark. The Dark Carnival is God, and Insane Clown Posse isn't sorry that they tricked us.

The Juggalos chant *"Fam-uh-lee! Fam-uh-lee!"* as they spread out across Hogrock to rage through the rest of this final night.

•          •          •

"Hey ninja, you okay?" a Juggalette asks, leaning over me and shaking me.

I jerk upright. "Yeah, yeah," I say, looking around me in a daze.

"Cool ninja, I just wanted to make sure you were alright," she says and goes off into the night.

Somewhere in the distance I hear the chanting of *"Fam-uh-lee!"* I passed out in a field of trash. To my left, the merch tent stands empty of its wares. Next to me lies my yellow backpack, containing my camera and empty water bottle. On the other side of me lies an empty bottle of whiskey. I have no recollection of how long I've laid here. A few Juggalos still mosey around partying, but not many. I get up, pack my stuff up, and walk the trail. I walk over the Drug Bridge, past the Tilt-A-Whirl, and into a big tent where I hear some noise. In this Big Baller tent, a 'lette grinds a pole while a DJ pokes at a computer. About ten Juggalos stand in the shadows. The only thing to look at is the young girl languidly twisting around a pole. Everyone is worn out—close to crashing; they milk these final hours.

"Hey, what's up, ninja? How's it going?" My eyes turn from the dancer and see Gore, the Ramen guy from the fire.

"Just chilling."

"Yeah, me too. You have a good time here?"

"Yeah, man, I did."

We look around the tent, the crowd dwindling down to just a few.

"I'm headin' back to my camp," I say.

"Yeah, I think I'm heading that way, too. I'm tired."

We walk out of the tent, through seas of trash, past the dark and gaping main stage, and past the wrestling stage. We walk together in silence, past the spray-painted porta-potties that say "Namaste sharts," past the empty autograph tents, past the merch tent, past the carnival games, past the Tilt-A-Whirl, past the Saturn 6, past Juggalo Jail, and past the seminar tent.

As we reach the exit and pass through it for the last time, I think of Eden. I turn, look back and see no angels with flaming swords guarding the gates of Shangri-La.

# SUBSCRIBE TO EVERYTHING WE PUBLISH!

Do you love what Microcosm publishes?

Do you want us to publish more great stuff?

Would you like to receive each new title as it's published?

Subscribe as a BFF to our new titles and we'll mail them all to you as they are released!

$13-30/mo, pay what you can afford!

*microcosmpublishing.com/bff*

## ...AND HELP US GROW YOUR SMALL WORLD!

*More gonzo journalism about weird music scenes:*